T0063110

THREE DAYS OF THE
CONDOR
OR FIFTY SHADES OF DRY

SECOND IN THE SERIES
FROM THE ADVENTURE LIBRARY

RANDY LIPPINCOTT

Order this book online at www.trafford.com
or email orders@trafford.com

Most Trafford titles are also available at major online book retailers.

© Copyright 2013 Randy Lippincott.

Cover photo—Crystal Davis on El Matador,
Devils Tower photo by permission of Simon Carter.

Printed in the United States of America.

ISBN: 978-1-4907-1443-1 (sc)
ISBN: 978-1-4907-1444-8 (hc)
ISBN: 978-1-4907-1445-5 (e)

Library of Congress Control Number: 2013917039

Trafford rev. 10/25/2013

Trafford
PUBLISHING®   www.trafford.com

North America & international
tollfree: 1 888 232 4444 (USA & Canada)
fax: 812 355 4082

IN MEMORY OF

This book is devoted to the memory of my father, H. R. "Dick" Lippincott, who taught me by example how to serve my country and be an honorable man, and instilled a sense of adventure in me. My dad believed in me. To Robert "Robin" Cox, my sergeant in Special Forces, who was my friend and helped make my educational opportunities possible. Also Col. James A. Webster, MD, who took me into his family and mentored me in the Nineteenth Special Forces. Robert "Bob" Hogan, MD, who supported me and gently gave me the confidence to practice family medicine as a Physician Assistant. To my friend and fellow adventurer Steve Steckmyer who made his final climb much too early. And lastly a heartfelt thank you, and all these years later, I still miss Mike Wasley, who befriended me and took me under his wing at the tender age of twenty-one when I was assigned to the Seventh Army Parachute Team in Germany. I have had some great friends and mentors on my travels. I love them and thank them for their unselfish involvement in my life. These men taught me the true meaning of serving God, country, and family. "What we are is God's gift to us . . . What we become is our gift to God."[1]

DEDICATION

As I've been swept down the river of life called civilization, my friends have been numbered. Sometimes mutual interests spark a friendship; other times I have been drawn by certain qualities or circumstances. Most of the people I've "known" have been mere acquaintances, not true friends. My closest friends have included schoolmates, skydiving associates, army buddies, and mountain-climbing partners. The following are significant friends that have most influenced me.

This devotion is to my very few treasured climbing partners: First in gratitude and chronology, **Terry "Lobo" Loboschefsky** for introducing me into the alluring world of rock climbing. He showed me that it was the journey, not just the summit, that we should value. We taught each other, mostly by trial and error, but Lobo was the inspiration and acquired the first rudimentary tools for the sport. Lobo and I made the transition from skydiving to technical rock climbing when we decided that the parachuting community was getting stoned in all the wrong ways. During those growing years, we practiced our rope tricks in a very cloistered environment, so we quickly reached a plateau. I loved the experience and camaraderie. Lobo only potentiated our relationship by laughing at my awkward attempts at levity. I grew to love the unspoiled range of physical and mental connection with the mountains and rock when touched in the sun and shade. We did diversify when Lobo signed us up to start ice climbing the winter of '76-'77. Now, as mountaineers, we continued to climb throughout the winters when ice conditions were favorable to maintain the momentum of the sport. Ice climbing was an incredibly different and challenging discipline, but all the same principles applied once I realized the gravity of the situation.

Early in our climbing exploits, I had a close call in Little Cottonwood Canyon. It was a mild winter, and we were dead set on a new route at Lisa Falls. After an uneventful climb in the wet conditions, we casually set up a rappel into the side canyon. Once I started over the edge and committed, I discovered that the rope was hanging free. My focus turned from the scenery to my situation when I realized that my lifeline ended 35 feet above the rocky floor. We had failed to tie a knot in the end of the rope, so I could have easily rappelled into a free fall and a messy death. I was able to swing on the Kernmantle rope enough to make contact with the rock face and climb back up to the rappel anchor and Lobo. We had just learned an important early lesson.

Left to right: Terry "Lobo" Loboschefsky and Randy Lippincott, Lisa Falls, circa 1975, "testing the waters." We made our own harnesses out of tubular wedding, rappelled off interlocking biners, and never gave a second thought to helmets. Photo by Randy Lippincott.

Later that summer, I helped start Lobo's family when I flew Paula Pazell and Lobo to a wedding reception in Garberville, California, on June 25, 1977. It was their first real date, and Lobo impressed her as my copilot in the Cessna Turbo 210. Our mutual love of flight has persisted over the years. Mine has been focused on utility whereas his has been mostly inverted. In 1979, I left the Wasatch for New York City and the Swangunks. I improved my skill level as I climbed with other people on both rock and ice. However, I never forgave myself for leaving Salt Lake City and Lobo because in my absence, he suffered a career-ending fall with a severe ankle fracture.

Randy McGregor, MD, enhanced my Alaskan experience both in quantity and quality. He taught me about the importance and organization of planning for a major expedition. I grew as an outdoorsman and learned the subtle nuances of fine camp life and the joy of simple pleasures in the wilderness. We developed a great camaraderie in cross-country skiing, rock climbing, mountaineering, ice climbing, and hunting. I always looked forward to the annual Valdez Ice Climbing Festival at the Andy Embic, MD, "climbers' hostel." The mountaineering slideshows and food at the Sandvik House were always fun and inspirational, if not mind-altering. Our trips together included more than climbing; we hunted Minto Flats, flew the Cessna 205 into the Alaska Range, and kayaked the Chena and Tanana Rivers in our Kleppers. Randy was the consummate outdoorsman because he effortlessly enjoyed nature and loved sharing his experiences with others of like mind. He had strong ethics for the environment and was always safety-conscious in the wilderness. Randy was a fabulous cook, and we always had gourmet food and fun together wherever we went. I do believe he introduced me to the fine art of meal preparation in the Dutch oven.

It was a thrill for me when I was with Randy on his first successful Alaska Range summit, Mount Hayes via the East Ridge. The Brooks Range proved to be an equal test of planning and judgment. As part of the group, he made the journey prudent and the total experience more fun. Randy's knowledge of the flora and fauna made our outings seem more like extra credit field trips . . . I still miss that.

Randy McGregor's first Alaskan summit,
Mount Hayes via the East Ridge. Photo by Randy Lippincott.

Kalvan Swanky needed someone to belay him in the gym, and
funny thing, so did I. It seemed as if we were both older than the
rest of the climbers in the gym, so we began climbing together by
default. Soon we had spent enough time together and developed a
rhythm to take it outdoors. Our backgrounds were both in traditional
(trad) climbing. Day trips at first, mixed with sport climbing, made
for many years of enjoyable outings and adventures. All the way
from Tahquitz to Devils Tower, Kalvan pushed me to beyond what
I thought I was capable of at my age. I may have complained then,
but I am grateful now. Kalvan's influence cast a wide net. He loved
to travel with me in my airplane and taught me that it was far better
to sleep indoors and that he not only knew which was the best wine
on the menu but most likely had a relationship with the owner of the

vineyard. Kalvan worked hard, but he liked to play hard too! I have done some of my most serious climbing with him. To what I thought was untenable Kalvan would simply reply with "Follow me, you can do it." He has never spoken an angry word in my presence or made me feel he was impatient with my performance. And yes, he too even laughed at my nonsensical humor and occasionally was the butt of some of my best practical jokes.

Outdoors is where Kalvan's judgment and skill shone through. He always seemed to know his own limits and never got us into a situation that compromised our safety on the rock. In his company, I was never avalanched on, froze an appendage, took a real whipper, or was struck by lightning. Some of us tend to learn our lessons the hard way. Thank you for the epic exposure and making the journey an enjoyable and secure one.

Kalvan Swanky on *Positive Vibrations,*
The Incredible Hulk, 2011. Photo by Sarah Malone.

AUTUMN SONG

Clear, unscalable, ahead
Rise the Mountains of Instead,
From whose cold, cascading streams
None may drink except in dreams.

(W. H. Auden)
March 1936

CONTENTS

FOREWORD by Kalvan Swanky

They say birds of a feather flock together, and it's true. Life is a fantastic journey, and it is made so much more fascinating by the passengers you choose to ride with along the way. I've been lucky to be blessed with a large number of great friends, but it seems as the years go by, you meet new ones a little less often. Randy was a happy exception. We met at the AZ On the Rocks gym after my other climbing partner moved away. I'm pretty picky about who I climb with since you can quickly get killed outside, and the partner ideally has to have a certain humor, wit, and calm manner in order to put up with the tedious parts of the sport (like hanging out for days together in a snowed-in tent). Randy appeared to be competent in the gym and seemed to know what he was doing. He looked a bit older than me but sure performed pretty well at pulling down! So hey, I took a chance.

That first day turned into many more training sessions and then, eventually, routes outside. The climbs became bigger and the trips longer and the friendship stronger. He shared a love for the outdoors, the spirit of adventure, and a desire to wrest every ounce of joy out of life. Randy really is the most interesting man in the world and pretty damn tough. When the time was right, he has told me some of the funniest stories I've ever heard in my life. He's had me laughing so hard I really think I did pee my pants (only a little). You'll learn some of the things he's done in his lifetime reading these fantastic stories, but you need to know this is only scratching the surface. I admire him in many, many ways. The world would be a better place if more men had his values and strength of character. It must be the farm-boy thing. (Man, I hate when Nebraska beats Colorado—my team—in football. He wears that dumb red Cornhusker shirt for a month.)

Enjoy these true-life tales from an authentic renaissance raconteur. He pours a mean Crown Royal on fresh-chipped glacier ice, can shoot the eye out of a hummingbird at two hundred yards and could amputate your leg with a rusty spoon, land a plane on a frozen lake during a stormy night, cook you the best meal of your life in the middle of the desert with a single pot, brew beer out of cactus juice, and make you laugh your head off.

Thanks for the memories, Randy; I look forward to more terrific stories and more great adventures with you.

PREFACE

My universe is no longer expanding. It was the best of times; it was the worst of times; I couldn't stop thinking how this story would end or if I could even write it. Does everyone think like I do—tangential, circuitous, just plain random thoughts, real or imagined? When deprived of water long enough, anyone will become delusional. Mirages in the desert, illusions of the mind—you only have to wait for the inevitable to invade your awareness of reality. The most helpless feeling is when you sense it slipping away and you know there is nothing you can do to right it except, of course, add water. You place your body on autopilot, relying on muscle memory; you divert all your energy to the absolute basics of vertical movement— focus, focus, focus! In the end, you feel feeble to the point of an irrepressible sickening feeling in the pit of your stomach. You secretly vow to never repeat this mistake too often duplicated in the desert. Most never live to tell their story.

In hindsight, had our judgment been clouded by a need for our next fix? Climbing can be a powerful narcotic. Psychology professor Bruce Ogilvie concluded in a study of risk-taking athletes, "They are simply 'stimulus addictive,' that is they have a periodic need for extending themselves to the absolute physical, emotional and intellectual limits . . . of psychic ecstasy found by living on the brink of danger." If the truth about climbing were known, you would realize a delicate interplay vacillating between fear and hope. Andrew Weil determined, "Tolerance is not a phenomenon associated only with drugs. In fact it looks as though human beings become tolerant to any pleasant experience that they indulge in too frequently." Please don't tell my wife!

It all started when Kalvan Swanky asked me what climbs I had on my "tick list." Although we had been climbing partners for a couple of years, I had never really thought about it before. I felt we climbed for fitness and fun. Sure, there were the desirable climbs from *Fifty Classic Climbs of North America*—Mont Blanc, the North Face of the

Eiger, and throw in K2 or the Moose's Tooth. No, I really didn't have a tick list of desirable climbs that I wanted to pursue. Since I had not yet reached retirement, my vacation time had been sparse, divided between family and other social commitments. I never really felt like I could make long-range plans for myself or afford it even if I did. It just never seemed to work out. Then there was balancing work with the discipline of training for a big climb and carrying a heavy load on my back. Subsequent to my lumbar surgery in 1973, I have always suffered back pain following a climbing trek with a heavy backpack.

We began to brainstorm. There were really no desirable multipitch classics per se in Arizona. It would be between Colorado, Nevada, Utah, Wyoming, and California. Kalvan knew Colorado well since he had gone to college and climbed there. We thought the Nose of El Capitan in Yosemite would be our final exam, but prior to reaching that, some good practice included the Exum Route on the Grand Teton; Devils Tower, Wyoming; Scenic Cruise, Black Canyon of the Gunnison, Colorado; Super Crack, Indian Creek; and Spaceshot, Zion Park, Utah. Oh yeah, throw in Figures on a Landscape, Joshua Tree; The Vampire, Tahquitz, California; and Crimson Chrysalis or Levitation 29 in Red Rocks, Nevada. I was dizzy just thinking about all the potentials. Combined, Kalvan and I had over sixty years of climbing experience. Were my expectations unrealistic? Could my body cash the checks that my ego was writing? I needed a giant whup-ass can of instant P90X.

This is a trilogy about three separate epic climbs with Kalvan. These stories may not answer why we climb but, rather, illustrate that as we allow ourselves to be tested by nature and cause us to reach into our physical reserves, we emerge the stronger for it. These are climbs that are difficult enough by themselves but were made more exhausting by the common thread of life-threatening heat. The insidious sun sucking energy, water, electrolytes, and even your willpower from a normal, healthy, well-conditioned man made the hard climb an even more grueling task. And Kalvan wonders where my dry sense of humor comes from.

In my subconscious, I secretly believed that my partner for the last nine years was paid to kill me. He would make it look like simple dehydration of an old geezer. It would not even warrant an autopsy. Who would have suspected any difference when they found the mummified corpse face down in the desert? They would never identify a weapon . . . or, for that matter, even a motive.

After years of climbing together, Kalvan has told me repeatedly that I am one of the toughest guys that he knows. When I put it all together in retrospect, I think what he really meant was that I am one of the toughest guys to kill that he knows. Routinely, I come home with the blood and scars to prove it. To throw me off, now I am the "Most Interesting Man in the World." Okay, the Dos Equis man— whatever. I think it was the alcohol doing the talking anyway.

These principal accounts, along with related stories of other climbs and near-death events that I have interjected, will depict three of our larger-than-life climbs: El Matador on Devils Tower, Wyoming, July 2005; Spaceshot in Zion National Park, Utah, April 2006; and Scenic Cruise in Black Canyon of the Gunnison, Colorado, July 2010. All three climbs share a common theme: one of repressive, severe heat in an extremely demanding, life-threatening high-stakes game. One in which we ran out of water and electrolytes well before the climb ended. Each outing exposed us to the relentless sun and record-breaking temperatures for that latitude and time of year. Skin baked, mentation slowed, swollen tissue, eyes blurred, lips chapped, tongues stuck to the roof of our mouths, painful calves that cramped, and feet that burned in geisha-tight climbing shoes. Not to mention the meat grinder that the hands were going through.

The most serious worry, of course, is when you stop sweating; that's when your concern increases for irreversible heat stroke and the loss of body-temperature regulation by the hypothalamus and all subsequent rational thought processes. It is a lethal combination in this vertical game. According to a recent issue of *Consumer Reports*, 650 people die each year in the United States from heat stroke. Heat illness is 100 percent preventable, according to the American College of Emergency Physicians.

Yes, our friend the California condor (*Gymnogyps californianus*) is a hideous vulture that silently circles high overhead, watching and quietly waiting for you to succumb and reach your last leg dehydrated and delirious as it patiently anticipates a large lifeless carcass on which to feed. The condor is a scavenger soaring great distances, spending days looking for opportunities, perhaps something the size of a fallen climber. Like the movie, *Three Days of the Condor*, our quest also lead us on a cat-and-mouse game (with Mother Nature) to discover our limits in a sport of endurance and the meaning of our mission, if we choose to accept it . . . a test of our physical and mental toughness. And just like the chiseled stoic vulture in real life, to survive, we had to be mentally willing to micturate on our own extremities for urohydrosis or succumb to the extreme heat and the menacing condor.

Randy Lippincott, 2013
Scottsdale, Arizona

ACKNOWLEDGMENTS

700 Sundays is a book and a one-man play by Billy Crystal. He relates to the limited time that he was afforded to spend with his father while growing up. It is a true-life, heartfelt, hilarious memoir. Like Billy, now I can quantitate the time that I spent with my father and wonder why we didn't make more memories together. But the time we did share was quality, and I loved my dad very much, and I cherish those times. He was my mentor and had shoes that I will never be able to fill. This is an acknowledgment of how special those seven hundred Sundays were, how he graced my life with his presence, and that his influence continues to this day.

First and foremost, I wish to acknowledge my father, who gave up the struggle on Tuesday, the twenty-eighth of July 2009. Without his gentle guidance and permission, I would never have tested the adventure waters. My dad's retelling of his boyhood escapades gave me the very basis for my enthusiasm and the possibility of high adventure. He retold tales of "stealing" the family car as a kid. Dad was an amateur pyromaniac when he set the grassy lane on fire "accidentally." He told stories of the family favorite team of horses— Maude and Florey. As a youth he acquired a pistol with his brother Dale that exploded when they fired it. "It could have put your eye out for heaven's sake!" He rolled a fully loaded beet truck as the rear wheels went into the ditch because he made the turn too sharply. In school shop, he built a magnificent model sailboat that made the landlocked yearn for the open sea.

Dad willingly volunteered for duty in the army during WWII and set an example for patriotism as part of the "Greatest Generation." He always spoke fondly of an interest in the possibility of his own motorcycle after discharge from the army, but life always trumped desire. However, Father did take the initiative when he purchased an airplane purely for recreation. He wanted to share his joy and skill with others, a truly uncommon endeavor for a small farmer at the time. Although he had the mechanical skills to operate the aircraft, it was a struggle for him to pass the written exam. It was only after his third try that he was able to take his check ride and earn his private pilot's license that served him without incidence until he retired it at age sixty-five. He was not a quitter and didn't shy away from a difficult task.

From a small farm in Nebraska, my first misadventure was totally unsupervised at age five on horseback. I developed a mechanical sense at age ten when I "worked" eight-hour days, driving the D4 Caterpillar pulling a five-bottom plow through the three-quarter-mile-long fields. My exposure to the idiosyncrasies of the maritime discipline came about that same time in a sheep trough on Prairie Creek. Next it was all things sports in high school, then a motorcycle at fifteen, and flying lessons at sixteen. I remember when my dad allowed me to play football even though his only brother was killed as a sophomore in high school playing the game. Only now can I appreciate how it must have torn at his heart to know the risk and yet rise above his own feelings, to *allow me* the choice. He would not dampen my vigor and determination for excellence. As an adolescent, one must test the waters and reach his own equilibrium. I had my father's permission at nineteen to begin skydiving and, like him, entered the army at twenty after one year of college. Father has been the comic relief for the family, the guiding light and the foundation upon which the family was built.

My schoolteacher mother set an example of placing pen to paper and has been a prolific writer. She wrote letters to me, both while I was away at school and in the army. She has documented her own life and experiences along the way. She has written her own volume, recorded her own thoughts, and chronicled her life and times for her children and their children. Possibly their children's children will be grateful to recognize and understand her struggles. They might begin to know the beliefs and feelings that were experienced during the life and times of Harvey Richard "Dick" Lippincott Jr. and Rosalie Jean Lippincott.

In retrospect, as I have matured, I realize that my parents have always been my best friends. Unselfishly they have always been there like silent guardians in the shadows, patiently waiting for me to beckon to them for assistance. No matter what my status in life or attitude toward them, no matter that I have not always risen to their expectations, I was made to feel worthy of their love and attention. For this I am grateful. They provided a wholesome environment that has helped mold me into who I am, and exposed me to many varied opportunities. According to Napoleon Hill, in his 1928 edition of *The Law of Success*, "the only lasting favor which the parent may confer upon the child is that of helping the child to help itself."

My parents nurtured me over the years and have helped this child help himself. This is a humble tribute to my loving parents. They have shown me by example, how to play the game of life. As role models they have influenced me and helped me through my growing years. They have been able to give of themselves when I needed and capable to graciously accept when I was able to give of myself. I have always tried to live by one rule: would my parents be proud of me if they knew what I was doing? As I look back on my life and recall my childhood, I would describe it as a mutual struggle—one in which we did not realize how much fun we were having; we were a farm family.

As a youngster, my dad held my forehead in the palm of his hand over the bathroom sink when I was sick, and I felt his love. The warmth of his firm, calloused hand soothed my agony as I repeatedly strained against it. And my mother placed cool washcloths on my face when I was feverish. I suffered a jamming knee injury when I jumped from a galloping horse at age five; I was comforted by my father as the doctor aspirated the blood from my left knee with the largest needle I'd ever seen. It was all OK, and I was unafraid. My anxiety was abetted by my father's presence. At that age, I believed my acute disability was from the dreaded polio virus.

Then my parents coaxed me through 4-H with fun and an occasional work project. They taught me the value of a dollar and that hard work can be rewarding. I sold fresh sweet corn along the highway from my dad's field for thirty-five cents a baker's dozen. I remember going straight to the bank and purchasing my first twenty-five-dollar savings bond and the little green savings passbook from Central Bank where I kept a record of my earnings. I remember paying cash out of that savings account for my first car and my first year of college.

My parents faithfully supported me every Friday night of my high school football and wrestling careers. My mom yelled louder and my dad felt prouder than any mother and father on the field or in the gymnasium. As a senior, with their support, I won a position at the state tournament my first year wrestling. They made me feel important. When I started flying at sixteen in the wide open country we call Nebraska, not many dads would have let a youngster pilot the family airplane all alone, but mine did. The rural way of life gave me a head start on many of my peers. My father taught me to respect and operate many types of equipment early in life. He gave me my independence, confidence, and skills to enhance my experiences.

I remember when, from out of nowhere, I was bitten by the skydiving bug. Yes, my father actually signed a waiver for me to start skydiving before I was of legal age. That consent must have weighed heavy on my dad's mind. I even convinced him to fly for me while I parachuted at home. Only years later did I hear from his own mouth that he would have flown the airplane straight into the ground if he had not seen my parachute open. My heart sank; my throat went dry and got tight when I heard him say that. I nearly broke down when I heard that spoken because I knew that it was true and not just words. I would have never placed a friend in that position. No wonder my mother had reservations about her flying for me to skydive. They gave me the freedom to take risks. I would not have grown or experienced new worlds without this flexibility.

When I decided to join the army in 1969, my folks did not resist, nor did they encourage me. It was a time of personal conflict, and it was a time of national conflict. I really didn't understand Vietnam but felt patriotic and was determined to find out for myself. I know they were proud to have a son in the elite Special Forces. They gave me the right to choose for myself, although the stakes were high and irrevocable. I remember when I decided to attend physician assistant school; I was encouraged by my parents. They let me know they approved and provided moral support. I was made to feel I was entering an honorable and worthy profession. They boosted my self-esteem.

Even when I started mountain climbing, they gave silent approval. The real test was ice climbing, and then came the stories of the infamous avalanches. They had severed the umbilical cord but proudly condoned my activities in a reserved fashion. My interests were their interests. My goals, no matter how trivial or eccentric, were their goals. They always made me feel I was the best, although I knew that I was only a struggling neophyte in whatever game I was playing.

> A man's best moments seem to go by before he notices them; and he spends a large part of his life reaching back for them, like a runner for a baton that will never come. In disappointment, he grows nostalgic; and nostalgia inevitably blurs the memory of the immediate thrill, which, simply because it had to be instantaneous, cold not have lasted. (David Roberts)

My wife, Joyce Berk-Lippincott, like my parents, is nonjudgmental and is consistently supportive of my efforts in life. She is my living angel and makes my voyage of adventure possible.

INTRODUCTION

This is a series of autobiographical climbing short stories and personal experiences. They are not intended to be a complete listing of my climbing encounters. Like most climbing essays, I will caution the reader that this sport is inherently dangerous and, in fact, may be life threatening. Don't attempt any such serious ventures without proper instruction, conditioning, and practice.

Unwittingly I started writing to document accounts of my exploits for friends and family. Early in life, my mother set the key example for this initiative with her first book. Following an outing with buddies, I frequently felt compelled to document the events on paper for kith and kin. Of course, many of these trips were never documented, but when inspired by the nature of the incident and to commemorate experiences, I wrote. Most of these stories have evolved in subtle ways over time, but the essence remains. All are actual episodes described in the most accurate detail as soon after the event as practical.

During my short existence, I have always returned to the mountains for introspection. It must be at least partially genetic for man to seek the "high ground," for protection, exploration, or an attempt at communion with a higher power. Occasionally the only reason is, "because it's there," but even Mallory expanded on this when he explained, "It is the struggle of life itself, forever upward. What we get from this adventure is sheer joy." But if we can look down on ourselves from above, from the proverbial mountaintop, often we may be more objective, if not more rational.

The ensuing mountaineering stories recount the pursuit of my pilgrimage, my coming-of-age. For me, climbing has been on an existentialistic level with my scuba diving, aviation, and skydiving careers. It seemed like my endeavor for the exceptional view and my own independence—truly a phenomenal golden period in my life. From Mount Whitney, California, to the Swangunks in New York, "a day not spent in the mountains is a day misspent."[2] I learned how I felt about my own survival when on many of those summits. In these stories, I strive to return to those times and mountains in search of truth on the rocky temples. This is the visionary perspective I seek. These accounts of rock climbing are about more than climbing rocks, it is about that one thing in life that truly sets you free.

CHAPTER ONE
Butch and the Sundance Kid

or the Crying Game

July 14, 2005, we scheduled time off, put together a gear list, and consulted the guidebook for Devils Tower in northeastern Wyoming. I was excited to attempt the classic but impossible-looking collection of sheer vertical pentagonal columns. It was hot in Arizona, but with only two of us and gear for our mission in the Cessna 172, weight was not an issue. We had visions of cool air and fair skies in the high chaparral of northern Wyoming. Kalvan Swanky met me at the airport, and we were off well before daylight. If Kalvan's brother Baron had come with us, he would have pronounced it "an emergency adventure!" How could you argue with that kind of rationalizing?

As we reached altitude and cool air, the airplane really wanted to fly itself. We winged toward Monument Valley and past Grand Junction, Colorado. Along the west slope, we made good time with light headwinds and decided to stretch our legs and take on gas in Meeker, Colorado, a quaint village with a scenic sloping runway. We refueled, had a bite to eat, and taxied out to take off the opposite direction that we had landed. When a runway is not level, the general rule is, land up slope and take off downhill. We had a great start to this far-off classic climbing destination. There was only one negative. In-flight service had been less than desirable on the first leg. I was hoping for it to improve on the next portion of our journey. However, instead Kalvan had a very restful nap.

All along the west slope we overflew manmade scars on the landscape, indicating gas and oil wells, in an otherwise remote unpopulated mountainous countryside. As we headed north into Wyoming, we were met with headwinds, consistent headwinds, consistent strong headwinds that buffeted the small aircraft with heated plumes of parched air. To get "under the wind," I flew at treetop level across endless dry oceans of swaying prairie grass and tumbleweeds, ever vigilant for the occasional untimely cell tower—we weren't looking for *that* kind of reception. The harsh blistering wind and incessant turbulence made for tedious slow work in the little aircraft.

There comes a time when you think, *Should I have driven?* The miles and hours dragged on. I glared at the GPS; it seemed like the numbers indicating the distance to our destination were increasing instead of decreasing. I felt this was akin to what the settlers experienced in their prairie schooners on the way west inching across this same endless expanse of virgin land. At last the control tower in Gillette, Wyoming, answered our call with permission to land. We were welcomed by the FBO and taxied to a transient parking space. Facing into the wind, we tied down the 172 before it was blown over. In due time, we unloaded the voluminous gear and secured a rental car. Now with air-conditioning, we headed to the village of Sundance, about sixty-two miles east, for a sit-down meal and some good rest.

The Wind Rivers

On the road, I was thinking of my first big climbing trip in Wyoming. It was the very snowy winter of 1981-82. That season I had been ice climbing with David Bjorkman from Salt Lake City. Both of us knew and loved the Wind Rivers and wanted to test our snow and ice skills in the wild. The Upper Tipcomb Basin fit the bill, and we planned the time off. A short four-hour drive from Utah found us in Pinedale, Wyoming, on a Friday night. Our rendezvous with the snowmobile insertion team came together as planned. This idea was formulated after our first failed winter climbing attempt in the Wind Rivers. As to not violate the wilderness area, we would only use the machines to the Elkhart Park area. Arrangements to meet at three o' clock the following morning were agreed upon, and we left to search for a motel. This was going to be our last night in civilization, and the two-man party deserved a warm, dry place to sleep. In comparable situations, it was usually the snow and our sleeping bags at the trail head.

Three weeks prior, I had made the same attempt with Dave without success. That fruitless effort had ended in an outright blizzard and bottomless snow. We scrubbed the effort after twelve backbreaking miles in the unforgiving conditions. At the end of that long day, we opted to cache our gear and make a second attempt when snow conditions improved. At the time we pondered the possibility of rodents feasting on five days' worth of food or dining on a $170 climbing rope because we had made the mistake of leaving salt on it from our hands. In the name of expediency, we were willing to risk the cache, not having to carry the same load over conquered territory a second time. This would also enhance our resolve for a return effort. Since Dave and I had been climbing together that winter, chances were good that we were going to finish what we had started.

Our snowmachine (snowmobile if you have never lived in Alaska) connection was a Pinedale local answering to the name of Bruce. Like others in the area, Bruce worked at a skilled trade, but in the dead of winter, there wasn't much activity. I asked a few questions on the first visit and soon located him at his favorite hangout—read that—tavern. Bruce met us with a wide-mouthed grin and a down-home handshake; he agreed that two cases of beer and a fifth of Schnapps would get him out of bed at 3:00 a.m. Naively I asked what kind of beer he preferred. Dave elbowed me in the ribs, saying, "PBR." Before I could get out a *huh*, Bruce's sleepy face again was overtaken by a huge smile as he pushed his nose into the air. Pointing to his hat, he said, "Pabst Blue Ribbon." Suddenly it all came into focus for me. The great American pastime . . .

As we tried to elude the omnipresent Murphy's Law, at 3:30 a.m., four sets of "bright eyes" had gathered at the Maverick gas station. We topped off fuel tanks and headed up the road to White Pine. The vehicles were parked at the ski resort; packs and climbers were then transferred to the iron dogs. As I left my car, I had visions of finding it buried alive on my return. We made good time to Elkhart Park and continued toward the wilderness area. Occasionally losing sight of the lead machine, thoughts of being thrown from the sled, not to be found until spring thaw, raced through my mind. We had, somewhat foolhardily, paid in advance!

At last the inevitable happened. As the hitch broke loose, I was instantly thrown forward into the sled on my equipment. The tongue burrowed deep into the snow for an instantaneous stop. Bruce, on the alert side after about seven miles of Arctic air, immediately noticed his load had lightened considerably. It didn't take long for him to maneuver his snow taxi back into position. In the magnificent black silence, we improvised a makeshift repair for the sled. Able only to pull the weight of the equipment, the machine roared off with all my life support gear in tow. I hardly had time to survey my injuries.

Alone I strolled down the snow-packed trail through the night, picking out familiar stars as though I were on Broadway, trying to decide on a play. Occasionally, using my headlight to identify the path, I caught a glimpse of the intrepid party ahead of me. When I arrived at the scene, all our gear was deposited neatly on the snow, and the machines were in position for the journey home. Deep powder snow in the backwoods blocked further advance of the sleds. Less than a mile from the wilderness area, Dave and I felt lucky to have made it that far in such a short time. As we turned to watch the taillights quickly disappear through the trees, a wonderful primordial silence fell over us. I enjoyed Dave's company and felt good about the upcoming adventure.

We peeled off a layer of clothing in preparation for what lay ahead and stepped into our metal-edged cross-country skis. Quickly we adjusted slender packs. In no time, we were easily gliding over the trail, illuminated only by ambient light, winding through the tall pine forest. Dave insisted I go first; he reasoned my eyes were better at finding the old tracks. I did not feel the need to use my headlamp, and after twenty minutes, my eyes had fully accommodated to the desolate darkness.

Miller's Park was a source of confusion on our last trip, and we didn't want to waste any time with costly navigation mistakes. Speeding through the looming maze of the forest, we entered a somewhat-familiar open snow-covered field. Carefully picking my way across the windblown surface, I sensed we were heading in the wrong direction. Suddenly I stopped; I explained to Dave that I believed we had just made our first mistake. We backtracked through the now-dim light where I thought the trail diverged, luckily placing us on the right path. I silently tried to remember the details of the Donner Party!

Now pushing on, we arrived in the Barbara Lake area (our cache site) three hours ahead of our previous schedule. We began to feel as though our preparation was paying off. Dave and I were working particularly well together. As we approached the hidden spot in the early morning light, I didn't recognize the trash on the snow. The remains of the food cache carefully packed for our return had been violated. I only noticed the equipment bags still hanging high in the tree. I anxiously shouted, "Our food has been eaten, all of our damn food is gone!"

Dave carried the scattered stuff bags to the trail; I scoured the area for remaining food as thoughts of storms like in *Little House on the Prairie* or, worse yet, *Alive*, crept into my mind. I found empty Ziploc bags here and there, unable to contain their morsels. A nearby mound of snow appeared to be a bloody battlefield as Wyler's red raspberry stained a large area on top, the rodent the apparent victor. Carefully assessing the food situation, we were confident our mission was not compromised. We divvied loads into equal weights and rearranged our expandable backpacks. Refreshed after a thermos of soup and a candy bar, we hit the trail in high spirits as though we were the Scarecrow and Tin Man blissfully heading toward the Land of Oz.

Lucky up to this point, we had made good time after entering the park by following three sets of day-old ski tracks. Scarcely five hundred yards from our cache, we came upon three sleepy-eyed travelers from Lander, Wyoming. They were the fellows that helped make the morning so easy for us. After a short visit, we discovered we shared the same destination, the Upper Tipcomb Basin. Joking about waiting for them to break camp, we were off plowing through deep snow transporting heavily laden bundles. We each took turns breaking trail in grueling snow halfway up to our knees.

When Dave and I cleared the pass between Hobbs and Seneca Lakes, the faster group quickly overtook us. The long lead across Seneca Lake was slowed by deep thick-crusted snow, made more difficult with oversized packs. The Lander party stopped to rest and take on water at an open spring near Little Seneca Lake. Indian Trail Pass was a good vantage point for a well-earned lunch. As we relaxed against sweat-covered backs eating leisurely, I pondered how well the nine-hour morning had gone. From this high point, we studied the Lower Tipcomb Basin and the path our route would take us. For the second time, we were overtaken by the Lander group. After a brief exchange and a challenge of a witty riddle to be solved before our next encounter, each member of the team quickly disappeared over the pass.

At last we mustered the energy to hoist sixty-five-pound loads onto sensitive backs and tender shoulders. From this strategic point, we knew our marathon fifteen-mile approach through forest and deep snow would be complete before nightfall. Compared to the summer route, our descent onto the ice-covered Island Lake would shorten the trail considerably. Unhindered, our skies glided over the fresh trail broken by the Lander group as we entered the Lower Tipcomb Basin. Visible in the overcast distance was the muted silhouette of our objective, the northwest portion of Mount Helen, framed in the distinct blush of alpenglow.

The rocky boundary between the Upper and Lower Tipcomb Lakes was an ideal place to pitch camp in gusts of up to forty-five miles an hour. The low-profile tent was sound, but it proved challenging to find adequate anchors. Wind-burned and drained by the day's march, we sealed ourselves into the blue-and-yellow nylon cocoon of our shelter. In a short time, we settled in for some hot food and drinks. Dinner was leisurely prepared over the next two hours as rehydration is a gradual process. We started with plenty of liquids, including soup and hot cocoa, later feasting on gumbo shrimp and rice that was pleasing to the pallet. Dave was easy company, and we were both in good spirits. We talked about the next day and that we should plan on another alpine start.

The scheduled climb dictated a 3:30 a.m. wake-up. Dave set his wristwatch alarm. Our vapor barrier liners kept us warm in our light down sleeping bags for a well-deserved rest. While sixty-mile-per-hour winds tugged at our aerodynamic tent, thoughts of uncontrollable skidding across the ice crept into my subconscious. I felt the possibility that at any moment, our shelter would break free of its moorings and begin to roll with us in it. I did not sleep well; I was anxious to meet the elements head on! However, I could hear Dave soundly sleeping, and soon I followed; although I was keenly aware of the extreme elements inches from the comfort of my sleeping bag.

After a good breakfast, we packed climbing gear and departed our base camp by 5:30 a.m. Everything took longer in the cold and hostile environment, but Dave and I worked together efficiently. In a light snow and now moderately gusting winds, we donned our skis and light packs with climbing gear, water, and food. North through the Upper Tipcomb Basin toward Mount Helen, the weather was going to be anybody's guess. The barometer was holding steady—it seemed to me we were receiving a friendly warning—but we pressed on. As we crossed the lake, our headlamps cast an eerie glow on the wind scoured exposed ice, revealing kaleidoscopic fissures and unexplained worrisome upheavals.

Breaking through the ice in these conditions was a death sentence. How could we know if a random thermal spring had thinned the ice and was ready to ensnare the unsuspecting traveler? Is that why Dave insisted that I go first? Propelled over the uneven slippery surface and jostled by strong gusts, I fought to maintain my balance on the ice. My entire world, defined by my headlamp, was an artificial horizon six feet in from of me. As I led on, it was hard to determine whether I was pushing my light into the darkness or, in fact, was it drawing me, possibly to my fate? I thought back on something that I had read, "If everything's under control, you're going too slow" (Mario Andretti).

My handheld Silva compass was my sole source of logic and guidance. The luminescent dial was energized by my headlamp and set for a course to our destination. I continuously speculated about what lay just beyond the reach of my light; my vivid imagination filled in any blank spots. Once we started to encounter boulders submerged in the snowy sea, we knew our pilgrimage was drawing to an end and we had reached the shoreline. At 10,500 feet, we left the slippery surface of the lake and began our northward ascent to the base of Mount Helen.

The subtle welcome light of morning became apparent as we made an eastwardly turn. Tower One jutted upward like a whimsical, sober monolith; distinctly separating itself from the rest of the sky. The rocky pillar thrust its spire upward, clearly visible, somehow escaping the white mist that so completely incarcerated the rest of the Upper Tipcomb. All at once, it became very personal!

An occasional parting of the early morning torrents to the northeast revealed the old familiar face of Dinwoody Pass. I had explored this valley the previous summer when I had climbed my first 14,000-foot mountain, Gannett Peak. It was something that I could say I shared with the pioneer climber Yvon Chouinard. It was also his first 14er. In its embrace only seven months earlier, I had firsthand knowledge of an old man's death in its stony grip. Although I had only a brief exchange with the weathered elderly foreign gentleman, I felt that he must have come home to die in peace as close to heaven as he could climb. In retrospect I believe that he made a conscious decision where he wanted to release his soul. I wondered if I would ever be so lucky to realize the same option.

Fleeting thoughts of doubt entered my mind. Dave couldn't explain why his partner had "lost his desire" the year before, making the same approach under much better conditions. Those words struck me with simplistic eloquence. This was a lesson of steadfastness for me that I never forgot. Winners don't quit and quitters don't win. Could the most demanding ice climb in the Wind Rivers have that kind of power? I didn't know, but I had the distinct feeling I would soon find out. My grit was already being tested by Mother Nature, and we had only just arrived.

The 1980 Sierra Club guidebook described the Tower One Gully as grade V, ice 5. It goes on with the following description of the climb: "A north-facing couloir between Towers One and Two appears especially fearsome when viewed from Dinwoody Pass. Containing ten pitches up to sixty degrees, the Tower One Gully is comparable in length and difficulty to the Black Ice Couloir on the Grand Teton, though it is never as hard as the latter's crux. Belays can be anchored with rock." This awesome description would replay in my head as our plans became reality.

While the icy windblown snow steepened, Dave and I stopped to strap climbing skins on our metal-edged skis. Digging the edges into the slope, strenuous, slow, steep switchbacks brought us to what was most likely the base of our climb. Full light was upon us now; it revealed what I questioned to be the best day for our ambitious ascent. Dave and I stopped to discuss our position briefly; I felt confident in his judgment and leadership.

As I reluctantly donned freshly sharpened crampons in the frigid windy conditions, I wanted to try a view a few hundred yards to the east to see if, in fact, this was our route. Dave rationalized Tower One was in full view and what was in partial view to the left obviously was Tower Two. The ravine, deductively, was somewhere in between. We were standing on a mountain of nearly fresh avalanche rubble that was at the base of some very significant gully. I wasn't sure if that was a good sign or not. Downrange at a shooting gallery was not my idea of a good time, even during a cease-fire. I did know that I didn't want to be there when the next deadly avalanche was triggered. I'm not sure if it really mattered that we were not wearing avalanche beacons. An avalanche like the one that deposited this amount of debris would have run us through a meat grinder and buried both of us in an instant. As I struggled with my crampons, observing what I believed to be threatening weather, the route appeared painfully indistinct to me. Convinced this was the approach, Dave led on as I finished securing my pack.

Unroped we started on a 40-degree slope approximately 60 yards wide at the mouth. Frequently I stopped to catch my breath; I found the postholing in the soft deep snow at nearly 11,000 feet tedious work. After approximately 200 yards, we approached a major fork in the wide gully. The left continued in a straight line; the right detour veered off at about a 45-degree angle. Unseen messengers beckoned to us from a flowing white road, disappearing into a cloud of confusion. As we worked our way up the Tower One Couloir in unison, resting after every other step, we were secretly delighted at embracing our challenge in full winter conditions! My mind continually toyed with the idea the worst possible environment existed just beyond my sight. And part of that ecosystem might include another serious avalanche.

Was there a hanging glacier or giant cornice out of sight waiting to share space with us? We very well may be the trigger for the next incontrovertible geologic event. Yes, you could say that I was gun-shy.

Concern was not remote as unmerciful continuous spindrift and mini-avalanches, at regular intervals, cascaded down on us, filling our steps as we lifted tired feet in machinelike aerobic fashion. At this point the snow was steep enough to allow the use of a single short ice axe (plunger fashion) in front of us as a self-belay. Using this method aided our movement and balance. It also added to the security of each step. The idea on the steepening slope was to be able to self-arrest before becoming airborne. Amid the meteorological chaos a calm mind embraced the surprising beauty of the couloir. Dave and I moved together, unroped in unison.

Although the route was never seen in its entirety, short sections hinted at what lay ahead. The steep couloir was reminiscent of the lake approach and our encumbered vision early that morning. Clean, sheer walls rose above us to the left and less severe rock on the right. Lichen on ancient native granite was decorated with heavy rime ice and a contrasting patchwork of drab colors. Guarded by unseen gargoyles, everything faded in and out of focus as the wind howled steadily, sapping our finite energy. Dave and I used nonverbal communication as we climbed in unison and moved closer together when necessary to speak over the wail of nature.

Finally I had to remove my glacier goggles as ice crystals were forced behind the lenses and summarily blocked my vision. Midway up the couloir, stopping what seemed to be hours of tedious step kicking, a glance upward through squinted eyes caught what was possibly the ridge top. I was convinced it was the bifid notch I had studied in my photograph taken from Dinwoody Pass last summer. I allowed this inclination only enough purchase in my mind to sustain the pace, never feeding what may be a false hope. Movement in the narrowing couloir intermittently eased as my crampons floated on steep, mature, hardpack snow. The angle of the gully was 60 degrees and revealed black ice under the occlusive white Styrofoam surface.

Now we were using an ice axe in each hand in concert with 12-point crampons on our feet. We both practiced our best ice-climbing techniques—kicking one foot at a time, then planting an axe, one at a time higher than its original position, in a very calculated rhythm. The firm snow was easy to penetrate, but frequently, the underlying brittle ice would "dinner plate"; a 12-inch disc of brittle ice exploded away from the surface after one or two blows. Although disconcerting, I knew that this was normal physics for black ice. This slowed progress and left you vulnerable until you secured the purchase of your axe with subsequent calculated blows.

I had learned to conserve my energy; ergometricly I allowed the momentum of the swing to carry the axe point deep into the frigid mass. First I needed to visualize a defect in the surface of the ice and then be accurate enough with my swing to strike it with the first attempt. I had to control my fear to control my movement. My focus must remain on the job at hand, not the consequences if I failed. We were still unroped at this point and had not stopped to place any rock or ice protection. We had already passed the point of no return. A slip and fall from this vantage would have ended badly on the rocks more than 800 feet below.

On steep ice, less than 60 feet from the top, I halted to cut a step on which to stand and for both of us to rest. It never occurred to us to get the rope out and place a couple of ice screws for protection. Maybe it was the altitude; maybe it was just confidence in our skills. This respite allowed Dave and me to discuss the last few unprotected moves of the climb. Dave argued that the left narrow chute rose to a higher vantage point; I conceded and followed close behind. The last few moves to the ridge top were made on mixed rock and ice. We smugly mounted the crest as though it were a stable favorite ready for a late morning ride! It was a rush of relief for me, but somewhat disappointing because the technical ice lay dormant beneath the veneer of firmly packed snow; we had just conquered the Wind River's largest invisible icicle! David Roberts described it as "the best moments lurk in the tension just before success." Pummeled by stiff wind and pelted by blowing snow crystals all morning, I was a sight for sore eyes.

Dave Bjorkman at the top of Tower One with a menacing view
of the route we had just climbed. Photo by Randy Lippincott.

My eyelids were nearly swollen shut, my cheeks cherry red and
puffy, and any exposed hair was ice encrusted. The moment was
captured on film, and we congratulated each other and savored the
victory. Almost unbelievable now, we carefully down climbed the
very steep top section, facing into the slope with an ice axe in each
hand slow-motion. This is a tenuous and most difficult maneuver
to perform safely. Unroped at this point, any errors would have had
terminal effects. I have never heard of anyone down climbing the
Black Ice Couloir on the Grand Teton. Once on less severe snow,

we removed our crampons and easily glissaded the remainder of the climb in quiet elation.

On the way out of the Wind Rivers, the weather improved for some spectacular winter scenery. Lightened loads made for a pleasant sojourn home on the well-established trail. We had accomplished our goal and safely concluded an honest wilderness winter climb. I was proud of our efforts and grateful that all our planning had paid off. I was already thinking about our next big trip.

Chapter One: Devils Tower (cont'd)

In the morning after breakfast, we proceeded directly to Devils Tower posthaste. I found my first views truly remarkable in the morning light. It was a colossal monolithic plug projecting vertically from the surrounding rolling grassy plain. Just like in *Close Encounters of the Third Kind*, one could easily imagine the parallel groves in the rock to be bear claw marks as described in the Indian legend.

> According to the Native American tribes of the Kiowa and Lakota Sioux, some girls went out to play and were spotted by several giant bears, who began to chase them. In an effort to escape the bears, the girls climbed atop a rock, fell to their knees, and prayed to the Great Spirit to save them. Hearing their prayers, the Great Spirit made the rock rise from the ground towards the heavens so that the bears could not reach the girls. The bears, in an effort to climb the rock, left deep claw marks in the sides, which had become too steep to climb. (Those are the marks which appear today on the sides of Devils Tower.) When the girls reached the sky, they were turned into the star constellation the Pleiades.[3]

About sixty-five million years ago during the Paleogene Period, the Rocky Mountains and Black Hills were uplifted, but the process was compromised by a lone plug of extruded magma. The rock mass

27

cooled into the hexagonal igneous upright columns that characterize this distinctively massive landmark. As cooling continued, these similarly formed massive parallel columns contracted, creating vertical cracks between them, ideal for climbing. Devils Tower was our nation's first national monument proclaimed by President Theodore Roosevelt in 1906 under the Antiquities Act.

Southwest corner of Devils Tower, Wyoming.
Photo by Randy Lippincott.

We registered with the park ranger, only to discover the north and northeastern portions of the tower were closed due to peregrine falcon nesting. Now we had to rethink our planned routes. The forecast record temperature was an unseasonably high 105 degrees Fahrenheit at the 5,000-foot elevation; so much for the cool northern latitude. Now all our options were in direct sunlight for the majority of the day. Let the baking begin. Climbing shoes on hot rock lose their inherent stickiness at high temperatures and increase the difficulty of the climb. Feet become inescapably hot and hands sweaty unless dipped frequently in your chalk bag. Exposed neck and calves burn if unprotected from the intense UV rays at the summit elevation of 5,112 feet. We yearned to scale something in the cool shade.

I wanted to climb the classic, but easy second free ascent route completed by Durrance in 1938. Just the name by itself was cool; the climb had to be awesome. Kalvan reasoned that we had not come all this way to do an easy climb. At last we decided on the unspoiled, clean lines of El Matador, the south end of the west face, a timeless and nearly perfect route (see the cover photo).

W is for Wild

Mount Whitney is wild and scenic and also has a classic imposing face but on a massively larger scale than Devils Tower. Proud, rugged, clean granite spires interrupted the sky. It was hard to grasp the beauty and the majesty with a single introduction. A completely foreign landscape to those not previously exposed to this perspective of such stark grandeur. As I flew the Columbia across the rocky face, it dominated the landscape, and there was no clearly visible sign of man from this perspective. Countless extremely unforgiving mountains punctuated with lakes and dwindling snow fields were all my mind and vision could register.

This was not only one mountain; it was an entire range of similar mountains running north to south. One massif was as rugged as the next; all competed for your attention. It was awesome but to be feared and respected—not conquered with kindness but brute force and cunning. In one giant sweep, it *was* Ansel Adams's *Yosemite and the Range of Light*. It was a grand canvas, all in various colors of subdued gray granite and corrugated shadows mixed with runnels of brilliant white snow. A truly sweeping landscape, it was God's cyclorama; no wonder it is included in the *Fifty Classic Climbs of North America*.

East face of Mount Whitney from the Columbia 400.
Photo by Randy Lippincott.

I picked up my nephew Sam Anderson that August 2011 morning at Lindberg Field in San Diego. My wife, Joyce, drove us over to Montgomery Field, where the Columbia 400 was parked, ready and waiting for us. I picked up my IFR clearance, and in short order, we were in blue skies on top and on our way to Lone Pine (O26). Eventually we cancelled our IFR clearance with LA Center and descended to 15,500 feet in preparation for a photo reconnaissance of the east face and our approach to Mount Whitney, the highest point in the contiguous United States. The weather had been forecast as mild and clear the next five days, and it looked like things were working out. The day highs in Lone Pine were in the mideighties with midfifties at night. The full moon was just starting to wane.

About six weeks prior, I received a call from a Physician Assistant associate at Mayo Clinic, Bill Perry. He had drawn seven permits for the traditional Mount Whitney hike starting on August 18. Bill planned two nights at Lone Pine camp ground, around 6,000 feet, then up to Trail Camp (12,000 feet), where he planned to base his summit bid. He developed this acclimatization strategy after his last successful summit undertaking of Mount Whitney. Bill invited me and two others of my choice. My immediate response was "You bet, I'll be there."

I started out with a call to my regular climbing partner, Kalvan Swanky, but he could not get a "hall pass." Next it was nephew Jon Lippincott in Arkansas; again he was indisposed, job hunting. My third call was to twenty-three-year-old nephew Sam Anderson in Cedar Rapids, Iowa. He was instantly excited and optimistic about taking on this new and exciting project. Over the next few days, I laid out my training expectations and equipment requirements. Sam was psyched and ready for the "emergency adventure."

In our preparation, I informed Sam that the standard eleven-mile hike may be our only possibility from a permit standpoint, but we could apply for a summit day pass with the potential of climbing the East Buttress. That means you only have twenty-four hours to do your business on the mountain. It seemed to be a daunting task. As it turned out, we made it to the ranger station in plenty of time. We obtained a coveted North Fork trail day pass (and wag bags, used to pack your own waste out) for the following day. It was only possible if Bill was willing to ferry us to the Portal (8,360 feet) at two the following morning. He cheerfully agreed. Our excitement grew, and I was reminded of a favorite quote:

> Mountains are fantastic examples of the power and mystery of nature, and the routes we climb on them are expressions of all that is best in the human spirit. (Michael Kennedy)

The airport courtesy car transported us to the close by Ranger Station, but when we headed up the mountain to check out the location and distance between Lone Pine camp and the Portal camp, it boiled over in Tremor Land. Sam said it was a bad omen, and he didn't want to get out of the car. We wanted to evaluate our logistics while waiting for Bill to arrive but felt lucky to get the car back to the airport (yes, it was all downhill, and I was able to turn around by letting the car roll backward onto a side road). Now at 2:30 a.m. in Bill's car, we pulled onto the main road from the Lone Pine campsite.

I noticed a single set of headlights way down the road toward town. In short fashion, Sam reported that it looked like a cop car—yes, and in fact, the red and blue lights were functional. After about twenty minutes of posturing, they let us off with a warning about taking the hairpin curves too fast and the consequences thereof. So far all our excitement had been with cars and cops, and not rocks.

Sam and I started hiking on the North Fork trail from the Portal at 3:06 a.m. It was crazy; uncharacteristically, I had only 1½ hours of sleep, but I felt good. My conditioning for the sojourn started in Coronado, California, at sea level. The first cardio was biking, and then I added dune hiking on the Pacific beach. With increased endurance, I added a thirty-five-pound pack to the hike until I was able to step it up to a dune jog with a full pack and a return run in flat loose sand. We divided gear the night before, and Sam was toting the lion's share. I had reasoned with him that I had the endurance, but my back simply could not tolerate a significant load for the over 12,000 cumulative vertical feet. By day's end, he knew who Sherpa Tenzing Norgay was and how he must have felt.

Soon we were passed by some day hikers on the main Whitney trail. In short order, we came to the second stream crossing with an old sign indicating the start of the North Fork Lone Pine Creek trail. Quickly it was steep but not hard to follow in the mystic darkness.

Moonrise was about 11:00 p.m.; by the time we were on the trail, it was nearly full and unobstructed overhead. Bathed in the divine light, it was surrealistic, somewhere between a murky dream state and an elixir for the soul. In the verdant deep forest, we could still see primordial pristine granite walls reaching high overhead to the boundary between rock and stars. Our senses favored the moist cool air along the cascading stream of the North Fork. Always present, it was more of a serenade than an annoyance. Our printed directions to follow the washed-out, poorly developed North Fork in the near pitch-black had been downloaded online, and we referred to it frequently:

The trail crosses the creek twice. The first time it is still a trail: if you find yourself scrambling against a wall, you simply missed the trail. Retrace your steps, look for a way to walk down (not up) to the creek and you should find the trail again. After the first crossing, the trail gets considerably steeper. The second crossing (when you head back for the northern side of the creek) is actually a triple crossing via three small waterfalls (depending on the season, they can be three or two or one, and they can be more or less wet). Once on the northern side again, you follow the wall upstream for about 30 meters. The trail ends abruptly against a narrow pile of rocks and vegetation. Face the pile of rocks in front of you and haul yourself up the rocks. Once you are up, turn 180 degrees, and walk downstream for 10 meters until you find a lonely pine tree that will help you climb up to the next level. This is by far the scariest part of the hike because you are on the edge of the (very deep) canyon. Look for the piles of rock (cairns) that mark how to avoid the edge of the canyon, that can be (and it has been) deadly. If you follow the cairns, you are likely to avoid too much exposure. You will be going up from layer to layer of rock (occasionally having to use your hands), until you regain the trail, which now proceeds steadily upstream. The trail follows the canyon of the creek. You are walking on the (Ebersbacher Ledges).

For us, this was all gained in the dark using our headlamps. No big deal, Sam did well; the description helped us focus on the route and kept us from the abyss. I was quietly thinking to myself, just who was Ebersbacher and how did he come to name these granite outcroppings? It sounded too much like the Hinterstoisser traverse on the North Face of the Eiger. That was mostly a sheer wall with dire consequences. At sixty-two, I wasn't prepared to embrace the White Spider. It tends to pump up the sketchy factor to the nth degree. I didn't say anything to Sam.

This takes you to the Lower Boy Scout Lake, which you have to cross (turn left at the sign No wood fires). The trail takes you to the other side (south side) of the lake and continues about 500 meters to a hill littered with talus rocks. You are likely to lose the trail because it hits the rocks. There are markers, but hard to find in the dark. You can simply make your own trail through the talus boulders, or look for the "use" trail that resumes after about 100 meters. This trail stays close to the vegetation to your right. If you can't find it, most likely you went too high (if you had gone too low, you would be bushwhacking). You may lose it again a little further up, but, again, look for it near the water. There is also a giant pyramidal rock that is a good reference point: the trail runs right below it.[4]

Rhythmically moving along the trail, ever upward, we were making good progress. Subsequently our senses were teased by the first rays of daylight and the associated diurnal temporary dip in temperature. We stopped for a drink and put on our watch caps for warmth. At Lower Boy Scout Lake, it was light enough for us to take a break, hydrate, and have something to eat. More and more of the stunning scenery was revealed to us, and it took time to process all of it. We sat, craned necks, took pictures of the waxing rays of light, and basked in the iridescent alpenglow. Dawn broke slowly over the Inyo Mountains to the east, throwing the silhouette and twinkling lights of Lone Pine into sharp contrast.

In daylight, we were soon off route (we detoured above the pyramidal gigantic boulder instead of below it, duh. Now we were on difficult steep slabs instead of the easy slopes along the stream below us, a real waste of time. John Wayne put it succinctly, "Life is hard, but even harder when you're stupid." In short fashion, we corrected our mistake after some penalty high-density bushwhacking. Once on the trail it was easy to follow as we saw other climbers descending, headed our way. The contrast in scenery made the route exciting in spite of the colossal vertical gain. The breathtaking views continually changed. We made the south turn and started the dusty switchbacks prior to Upper Boy Scout Lake. We easily traversed the next dry valley above its lateral moraine and mounted the last steep ramp to a large plateau and the lake. Soon we could see Iceberg Lake (12,696 feet) and the intimidating full east face of Whitney in the dazzling sunlight. It was just after 11:00 a.m., eight hours into our day trip.

Sam and I approached some friendly climbers for beta that had just come off of the East Buttress. Thoughtfully, I suggested to Sam that (1) Iceberg Lake could be our objective and we may leisurely return to the Portal and join Bill and friends for the traditional route up—this was quickly vetoed; (2) go for the East Buttress climb and plan to bivouac in the open somewhere on the way down; it would simply be too late to try and rush the climb, be tired, and risk poor judgment and injury on the descent; all, of course, would have been in violation of our North Fork day pass; and (3) we could cache our gear, take water, helmet (for potential rock fall), and jackets and easily complete the northeast steep couloir in four hours. It was agreed; this would meet our goal of summiting and put us back at the Whitney Portal well within the twenty-four-hour time period.

As we set out for the Mountaineers Route from Iceberg Lake, a few friendly clouds started to form in the sky. We made steady progress up the steep scree slopes until Sam had to call a halt due to epistaxis (a nosebleed). In our Spartan style, we delved into our wag bag accessories and treated his nose with tamponade from the rolled-up corner of a baby wipe. Now at the top of the notch, we made a 90-degree left turn up vertical blocks and some ice-covered ramps to the huge summit area. This approach remains unchanged from John Muir's solo first ascent via the northeast steep couloir. That route was not repeated for more than fifty years following his 1873 offensive. Normally used as the climbers' descent, it was much later named the Mountaineers' Route.

On the peak, there were easily thirty hikers milling around. We were clearly identifiable since we were the only ones wearing helmets. In the nearly calm air, we heard someone remark, "Where did those guys come from?" The vista was as advertised, clear and unrestricted, but not quite able to see the curvature of the earth. However, my panorama included the sierras all the way to Yosemite. Comprised of huge, mostly flat boulders, the summit was nearly 100 yards square. We quickly found multiple official benchmarks near the predominately eastern view. In the center sat a large stone hut erected in 1909 by the Smithsonian Institution. This was fashioned to house members studying the planet Mars for water vapor; this included members of the Percival Lowell Observatory in Flagstaff, Arizona. Brisling with lightning rods, the tin-covered primitive structure had bombproof steel shutters for the windows and a well-used chimney. It stands today as an emergency refuge to intrepid hikers—rugged and little changed by time and the elements.

We took the requisite peak photos, did some people watching, and I started to look for the exit cairns. I was thankful that we were doing it in full light, dry rock, and no threat of lightning! Sam wanted to savor the moment and extend the summit event. I reminded him we had only come halfway and had miles to go before we slept. After a couple of attempts, we decided on the exit ramp and started to carefully pick our way down the very tenuous and icy exposed rampart.

Left to right: Randy Lippincott and Sam Anderson in front of the summit hut on Mount Whitney, California. Photographer unknown.

Back at Iceberg Lake, the nearly four thousand vertical feet round-trip had taken us three hours and forty minutes (including our fifteen-minute summit tryst). Now we took time to eat, drink, and soak our tender feet in the freezing water, a mechanical anti-inflammatory. We retrieved our gear carefully hung on sticks from large boulders to protect it from the gnawing teeth of the local marmots. In an unhurried fashion, we made preparations for the return trek and set out at about 3:30 p.m. Sam and I both were in good spirits and felt good. No headache or symptoms of altitude sickness. Except for minor wear and tear on Sam's feet and nose, we were both in perfect condition.

Refreshed by the lake, invigorated by the summit, our stride was lighter on the now-familiar trail. We passed parties both going up and down. We met young and old, male and female. Downhill was easier, but after all, it was a rugged sixteen miles and over twelve thousand vertical feet round-trip. Gravity is an awesome thing. Like the stallion returning to the barn, our step was slightly quicker and our attitude more positive. We were racing against time, but we no longer considered darkness a hindrance, and we knew what our pace should be. We met our goals, and followed the rules in good style. I was reminded of a quote from Royal Robbins, "that life is an adventure and that character counts." It was really fun getting to know my nephew, and I liked him.

In the dwindling light, my wrist altimeter seemed stuck. My knees were fine, but my legs were starting to tire. When you fatigue, you may misstep. When you misstep, you may twist your ankle. When you twist your ankle, you may lurch forward into a boulder or off a ledge. We made several wrong turns, had to backtrack narrow exposed ledges uphill, and bushwhack along the stream to find the trail. I guess it could have been worse. Now on the jet-black path (it would be nearly midnight before moonrise), we made telephonic contact with Bill for the Portal rendezvous. The trailhead was a welcome site, dark, just the way we had left it seventeen hours prior.

When our ride arrived, we returned to Lone Pine camp and sustenance. We were well hydrated, and I did not feel all that hungry. We rolled out our sleeping bags on the ground and quickly fell asleep.

At 5:00 a.m., Bill woke us for the shuttle to the airport. On the way, we stopped at McDonald's for an Egg McMuffin and some coffee to go. By 5:45 a.m., we were loading the Columbia for our return trip, and Bill was well on the way to start his hike up to Trail Camp.

Sam and I loitered at the airport, taking in the vast scenery and basking in the memories of the past twenty-four hours. I finished preflighting the plane, and we asked about a French Citation jet parked next to us. As it turned out, he was the owner of Crystal Geyser Water Company. The production plant was nearby, and he was in town checking on his operation.

Subsequently, Bill told me he did not summit. His party insisted on stopping at Outpost Camp (10,365 feet) instead of the planned Trail Camp at 12,000 feet. This took away the elevation advantage of the higher camp for the summit bid. Bill felt he was compromising the chances for the rest of his party to summit when he hit the "wall" at 14,000 feet. Since he had been there before, he told his brother-in-law Bill and Jamie to continue without him. He waited for their return prior to heading back to Outpost Camp and the ninety-nine switchbacks. On departure, we took additional photos of Whitney's ninety-nine switchbacks as requested by Bill. It was a smooth ride home accompanied by "The Blend" on XM Radio, and we shot the ILS approach at Montgomery Field. Joyce picked us up, and Sam and I had plenty of time for a little saltwater sailing in San Diego.

Chapter One: Devils Tower (cont'd)

The approach to El Matador was via a two-mile-long paved sidewalk that encircled the entire monument. Off the path was a short hike through the woods; and several hundred feet of large boulder hopping, scrambling, and negotiating fields of scree that led to sheer columns. All of this was debris from thousands of years of exposure to ice, wind, and sun. Geologists calculate the last column fell ten thousand years ago. What we were viewing was the result of igneous attrition. The climb was continuously visible, and my excitement grew. It was simply an incredible formation. It was, in fact, a national monument, and we had been given permission to complete the climber's communion. We sorted equipment at the base of the route, geared up, tied into the rope and I started off. Kalvan belayed and carried a small pack with tape, water, power bars, and trail mix.

The first short easy section (5.8+) was a sweeping column to a large platform. I used an easy layback technique while the climb was still in the shade. At the end of this pitch was an austere podium where Kalvan organized the rack for efficient pro placement. What was coming next would be demanding, continuous, and awkward as hell for me and my short legs. This pitch would test my climbing skill and Kalvan's patience. We may still be in the shade, but it wouldn't last long and the temperature was rising.

Dreamus Interruptus

My suffering hasn't always been by consent, but I have volunteered for some hard knocks through the years. My father's nickname for me was Butch. He said I was small but was the toughest of the "litter," and the name seemed suited for me. I think he had first heard it used in the army. Being wiry with a can-do attitude will make up for a lot of size. As I climbed, I flashed back to my childhood helping my dad move irrigation tubes at 2:00 a.m. and suffering through midday muggy heat loading sixty-pound bales of dusty hay on the farm. I remember summer heat that could scorch the pursed lips and tongue if you sucked in for any period of time. Dirty, grimy, and sweaty, they were my growing years and we worked hard, but my dad paid us. I wanted to use the seventy-five cents an hour that I earned in 1964 while working for my father to purchase a motorcycle. At last I had the $460 to buy a new white Honda 150 Dream motorcycle. I had grown up alongside the highway and knew the rules of the road. I also had driven a three-wheeler and the family car on the county roads, but without the practical experience of driving on the blacktop, I made a near-fatal mistake.

On an overcast windy Sunday afternoon, I made an impulsive U-turn on the two-lane Prairie Creek Bridge on State Highway 14. As it turned out, it was in front of a late model very large Chrysler New Yorker passing me at the legal speed limit of 65 mph. While driving into the wind, the locknut on my mirror vibrated loose, and I was unable to secure it with one hand. I was sure that I had checked and there was no traffic behind me. As I crossed the white line, I looked up as the massive car came into focus. It was in ultra slow motion as my mind raced to debate and explain the out-of-place supernatural vision I was witnessing. Just what was occurring? I really thought it was some kind of cruel weird joke! Surrealistic . . . this simply could not be happening to me; it was unadulterated denial. I could clearly see that it was a car unavoidably bearing down on me at a very high rate of speed in my lane. No time for even an "Oh shit!"

There was simply no escaping what was to come next. I could hear the tires screaming on the dry pavement for a fraction of a moment, then nothing but white light with the sound abruptly turned off. That's where my story could very well have ended and most likely should have. Unconscious and airborne, my body was ejected thirty-five yards off the highway bridge. Like a rag doll or, better yet, a lawn dart, I landed on a sandy beach far below the overpass. I believe the back of my head was cut open on impact when the arc of my flight was abruptly intercepted by a lone piece of concrete on the riverbank.

I didn't come to until I was again standing over my still-running bike. What had just happened? I turned to see the car 50 yards down the highway twisted 180 degrees counterclockwise, still pointing at me. The left front fender was crushed into the wheel and made the vehicle undrivable. The elderly motorist came over to assist me and escorted me back to his car. First he asked if I was all right, and I told him I was OK. Next he held his arm up at a forty-five-degree angle to indicate my witnessed flight path off the motorcycle. Mathematically my apogee was fifteen feet above the bridge but thirty-five feet above the riverbank below.

We waited there for help. While in the car, I noticed the dampness of blood on the back left side of my neck. I carefully teased a two-inch flap of scalp with my left index finger to feel an intact skull. It was as if I was examining someone else's wound. It really didn't hurt. All I could think about was that my dad was going to kill me when he found out that I had just wrecked my brand-new bike. When I pulled my finger back, I was thankful not to see any gray matter or bony fragments. Mother drove me to town to have my head x-rayed and my scalp sutured. I really felt OK at the time.

My parents consoled and cared for me in my time of need and soothed my cuts and bruises without the threat of criticism. Later I learned in my Special Forces training, what doesn't kill you makes you stronger. Although I was able to walk away from the crash, when I awoke the next morning, I was literally paralyzed with pain. Every muscle in my body screamed out in protest; it was like nothing I had ever experienced! I was unable to move from my bed. Yes, it felt like I had been hit by a train! Time was the only thing that was going to heal my injuries. My small frame had been insulted by the forceful and traumatic acceleration from zero to 65 mph in .4 nanoseconds. I had miraculously ricocheted off my bike and was ejected from the bridge; I had just experienced my first free fall and, unfortunately, my first concussion.

Some sixteen years later, I stopped at the family farm in Nebraska on my way from New York City to Salt Lake City. I casually returned to the bridge and the scene of the accident. That day, as I retraced my path and thought back on the details of the "thrill ride," I experienced déjà vu. I had just recovered the black box from the accident after all those years. Yes, I had an epiphany; it just came to me! It's like it was there all along but repressed. I remembered the indelible image of the car bearing down on me, the ever-so-brief instant of screaming tires on the blacktop, the complete absence of impact, the very bright white light that enveloped me, and then I recalled, for the very first time, getting up from the sandy beach, zombielike, and crawling up the steep grassy slope to the blacktop on my hands and knees.

I instinctively walked toward the sound of the motorcycle that was still running, and standing over it, like in the opening scenes of *Saving Private Ryan*, I slowly started to become aware of my surroundings. Gradually my senses, one at a time, were coming back to me as I recovered from the impact. To me, it looked just like a giant had stepped on my new motorcycle and it was in the throes of dying as it was still chugging in first gear. Reflexively, I knelt down, grabbed the mashed key, and switched it off. Much later in life I realized that I had a full-time angel watching over me. You would feel the same if this is what had happened to you. I'm no cat with nine lives, but I remember my dad always told me it's better to be lucky than good!

Chapter One: Devils Tower (cont'd)

Pitch two of El Matador was the classic definitive box stem ad infinitum. Although rated 5.10d/11a, it is far easier if you have longer legs than mine. One is held securely in place by pressing an outstretched foot against opposing columns, vis-à-vis the splits; your pelvis and gravity does the rest. Pro placement can be managed almost anywhere in the crack on the left side of the chute. Cams or wired nuts were bomber placements. There are good hand jams and finger locks, but sustained agonized stemming was the key. When I was able to execute this maneuver, I could only manage painful inches at a time. I was at my very limits. There is simply no way to think your legs longer than they are. This powerful waddle motion was akin to watching an inchworm on greased glass—with considerable effort, I was going nowhere fast.

It was an endurance struggle that eased somewhat near the top due to narrowing but was otherwise unforgiving. No crux, but no breaks either—one of the most classic and aesthetic climbs I had ever been on (cover photo). Kalvan lead this full-value pitch with occasional grunts and sheer determination. Gravity, stemming at my very limits, and the left-handed crack were my only consistencies. My hamstrings were the first to cry out in spasms and agony. Why was I trying to detach my adductors with this unnatural act? I frequently had to resort to strenuous lie-backs and jamming toes in the unforgiving corner. This was the only relief I had from doing the splits. My mind and body were unalternately fixed to the task at hand.

For me an adventure is something that I can take an active part in but that I don't have total control over. (Peter Croft)

Kalvan Swanky leading on El Matador, Devils Tower, Wyoming.
Photo by Randy Lippincott.

The third pitch started with a near-vertical hand crack (5.8) about 40 feet in length. It ended in a large belay ledge and two welcomed bolts for solid anchors. This is where taping my hands paid dividends; admittedly cracks have never been my forte. The hand or finger crack can cut sharply into the bony areas of the fist or peel skin from a digit if not done properly. Occasionally I had to hang my entire weight on a single point of contact. If this were over a crystal, it might as well have been a drill or ice pick digging into my flesh. Once injured, it's like walking a long distance with a rock in your shoe; the insulted area is repeatedly battered and becomes sensitive to the point of distraction. It turns out to be a very unwelcomed and bothersome hitchhiker.

On the Rocks

My serious work as a climber started in 1982 when I took up bouldering to become a stronger and more proficient rock climber. The following is a description of the first difficult problem that I mastered.

As I stood beneath the enormous slab of granite, my palms were damp with anticipation. Before me was a vertical 12-foot face; an imposing roof near the top was the most challenging part of the climb. Any hesitation could result in a backward fall and possible injury. Like a sprinter before the race, I nervously shook my arms and legs, awkwardly trying to remove "cobwebs" from my psyche. Mechanically I reached into the gymnastic chalk bag attached to my waist to dry my calloused fingers.

First I inspected the granite as I began to visually embrace the monolith for the communion to follow. I studied my footholds as my outstretched hands searched for subtle depressions in the unyielding mass. My start was as tenuous as I knew the finish would be. As I ratcheted up questionable fingertip holds, I kept my arms straight in order to allow my body to hang away from the rock; this mechanically forced my toes onto tiny perches and gave me traction. I pulled my body upward, selecting higher footholds until my hands were chest level. Delicately I slid my toe against the rock for steadiness and flagged my leg for stability; my fingers began to feel the strain. With a burst of energy, quickly but decisively I mounted the overhang. As to not lose momentum, I forced the bulge.

Now delicately I searched for invisible holds; my fingers hooked welcome micro flakes in a static fashion. As I balanced, straining on the apex of the roof, the hazard filled rocky ground beaconed from below. I eased upward, extending my tense neck, gaining a purchase with my free hand on a small but solid crystal, the size of which allowed me to hang on only my index and middle fingers. The sharp stone tore at my calloused fingertips. My right hand locked into a clawlike grip, I felt my forearm muscles attempt to free themselves from their bony attachments. At any instant I could become airborne.

As both hands strained, both feet "toed in," each athletic move tested my core strength. Already swollen muscles started to ache with a lactic acid buildup equivalent to fifty pull-ups. I concentrated all my energy on the crux; slowly I moved, allowing my feet to fluidly dangle in free air, forcing rock into flesh. In a last surge of energy, I sprang like a coiled snake. Dynamically I strained, my feet landing where my hands were—*pied à main*. At last I stood erect, the victor. A great sense of satisfaction welled up inside me, and I knew I had done what the average man could not.

Randy Lippincott practicing a classic strenuous bouldering sequence in Little Cottonwood Canyon, Utah, 1982. Photo by Cathy McCalman.

Bouldering is a blend of rock climbing, yoga, gymnastics, and ballet. It is a less well-known form of short rock climbing and means "to literally climb boulders." They may be small enough to reach over with the challenge of a single move or several stories high with a real commitment for even the seasoned climber (referred to as high balling). The difficulty of the moves and seriousness of the landing should be matched to the ability of the climber. The uniqueness of bouldering is that one may progress at his own speed to his highest level of ability. By gradually pushing your own limits and improving style and techniques with practice, you are able to overcome psychological barriers and build strength. Bouldering allows one to start climbing naturally by staying close to terra firma.

Why boulder at all, you may ask. For some, it is the first step in a natural progression, a means to an end. Others may use it as a warm up or for mental preparation. Dave McAllister describes bouldering this way: "For those brief occasions . . . you are your own memory's blacksmith. Things are not happening to you. You are making them happen." Playing in the boulders may also be an end in itself.

Master boulderer John Gill, in Pat Aments's book *Master of Rock*, comments on bouldering: "It is the accomplishment of something physically very difficult. It is a distillation of the acrobatic part of climbing and hence, only a part of the actual rock experience. To a great many rock climbers it is precisely what it has been traditionally, and that is, a form of training."

> For many years, bouldering was commonly viewed as a playful training activity for climbers, although in the 1930s and late 1940s Pierre Allain and his companions enjoyed bouldering for its own sake in Fontainebleau. The first climber to make bouldering his primary specialty (in the mid-1950s) and to advocate its acceptance as a legitimate sport not restricted to a particular area was John Gill, a mathematician and amateur gymnast who found the challenge and movement of bouldering enjoyable.[5] John took bouldering seriously and could demonstrate with a one finger pull up.

Many boulder for different reasons; some of these may be convenience, accessibility, and variation. Bouldering can be more suitable than longer technical climbs because little equipment is required. This type of climbing is typically a series of a few difficult moves and is done without the aid of ropes or standard rock protection. Climbing shoes, gymnastic chalk, and occasionally, a crash pad are generally all that is used. Bouldering is also convenient because a climbing partner is not necessary, and it is possible to attempt a difficult move or a different route on the boulder more than once in a very short period of time. Accessibility is important in bouldering. Boulder fields are often easier to reach than full climbing routes. This makes short workouts on the rock possible in a minimal amount of time.

One of the best things about bouldering is the mixed climbing it affords. Bouldering may be as varied as multipitch technical climbing, requiring the skills used to climb cracks, chimneys, and faces. One may test his strength, stamina, balance, or his ability to solve difficult challenges. Strenuous boulder problems may be conquered with a given sequence of moves for a short individual, while someone taller may bypass his key moves. Paradoxically size may make it more difficult to unravel the problem because of a high center of gravity. Often women are better climbers than men, have just as much endurance, and are sometimes better at problem solving.

The objective of bouldering is not in reaching the summit but, rather, "solving the problem with style." When learning a difficult move, a lunge may become necessary, but with practice, the same dynamic move may be done statically. With increasing confidence and ability, bouldering takes on a graceful, flowing nature. The proficient boulderer makes the moves appear effortless. Jeff Lowe remarked in *The Ice Experience,*

> There is certain purity in engaging in what some would call a useless activity. When the climber confronts the overhang, he does so with the knowledge that no material gain will result from the completion of the task. Yet he commits his whole physical/mental/spiritual being to climbing the bulge. He is confident that when he is done, the satisfaction will outweigh the effort.

Along the same lines, Colin Wells elucidated, "That of course, is the paradoxical allure of adventurous mountaineering: The game is worth far more than the prize."

For some, climbing or bouldering may be a release, a confidence builder or a challenge, while others scoff and regard it as taking unnecessary risks. According to DuPont, perception of risk is a function of three factors: (1) perceived individual control, (2) familiarity with the consequences, and (3) sensationalism and magnitude in terms of human loss. Individual control in this case is as much mental as physical. Although one may be strong enough to maintain a purchase on the rock and move to the next hold, one is unlikely to do so without confidence. Telling yourself you will fall, you fall. In youth, we usually become aware of the consequences of falling a short distance, usually off our bike or the roof. A broken arm or sprained ankle was part of growing up, and the consequence was only one of inconvenience and life experience. As ultimate TV watchers, most people have become desensitized to human loss.

Therefore, the risk of bouldering can be easily rationalized by the climber and accepted in a progressive steplike fashion. Nonclimbers often marvel at the monolithic gymnast and wonder how they grow to be gracefully masochistic. A person today enjoys more free time than any other period in history. New technology has allowed us to entertain ourselves from the depths of the ocean to the surface of the moon. However, the real escape is for the boulderer, who is preoccupied with clinging to the massive object, lost in time as all other thoughts fall away like chaff to the wind.

> Newspapers ascribe the word 'climber' to any person who falls in the mountains or off a rock. To refer to anyone who falls in the mountains as . . . a climber . . . is as factual as to say that anyone who sits down at a piano is a pianist. (Pat Ament)

Granite's the stuff; I can't get enough.

Chapter One: Devils Tower (cont'd)

The fourth pitch on El Matador was about 90 feet long that started at the belay ledge. We hand-jammed the left crack for about 15 feet until we came to a pin. Then we traversed hard right to a second crack up to a roof protected by small wires and a small cam. The crux (5.10a) was facilitated with tenuous finger locks, then another small roof and a short crack (5.9) to the belay stance, and two bomber bolts for anchors. Now it began to feel airy. It was an exposed area well up on the west face with a view to match. Now just what were those Indian maidens thinking, anyway?

The last pitch was easy blocks and cracks with unattached holds of all sizes. Care was taken not to dislodge any loose rocks onto potential climbers below us. The route topped out with a few unceremoniously easy moves. The summit was like a large rocky meadow floating in the blue sky, but Julie Andrews was nowhere to be seen. One had a sense of being in a truly pristine, sacred Native American place. We removed shoes from blistered sweltering feet, drank our last precious drops of water, and briefly explored the unique summit. After photos were taken, we headed for the rappel station. We did meet other climbers on top but weren't prepared to hang around due to the lack of shade. This scorching-hot, unforgiving landscape really redefined the word *Sundance.* It had been a real sense of achievement in a unique setting and a spectacular rock formation. A mystical feeling came over me as I envisioned the long and varied history of this unique spot. We didn't plan to linger in the 105 degree heat!

We rappelled down the west face next to our climb. Once back at the base of the massif, our second objective was Mr. Clean (5.11a). Due to fading energy, we only climbed the first pitch, which was long, continuous, and difficult. We felt that we had reached our objective and hiked back to our car and drove into town for dinner. Yes, we were tired, hungry, and parched after a long extremely hot day. Once in the Sundance Bar, we ordered a couple of ice-cold beers. Between the altitude, physical stress, and dehydration, our blood alcohol levels instantly skyrocketed. It literally could not have been faster if we had injected it intravenously. Neither of us had experienced this kind of sudden high brought on primarily by thirst. Kalvan and I both looked at each other and thought, *Are we cheap dates, or what?* Following a hearty cowboy grub supper, we staggered back to our hotel, showered, and collapsed into bed. My legs quivered once in the horizontal, and my hamstrings spasmed under the sheets. The repeated "wishbone maneuver," stretched my thighs beyond their designed limits. With patience, a hot shower, and Advil, sleep came.

The following morning, at a reasonable hour and after another good dose of Advil, we set off for Gillette and the waiting 172. I had contacted my dear friend Senator Bill Hawks in Casper, Wyoming, and he agreed to host us for the night. We spent more time in the bumpy 172, nap-of-the-earth, some of it crabbing sideways in the stiff wind. Now why did we have a headwind traveling both directions? Bill and Jan met us at the airfield in their Suburban. They graciously took us to their ranch house for a shower and change of clothes. After the white-tablecloth steak dinner, back at the house there were stories and drinks until the wee hours. No one is more gracious and makes you feel more comfortable in their home and in conversation than the senator and his hospitable wife.

Overstuffed beds, down comforters, and crisp sheets made us feel special and guaranteed a great night's rest. After breakfast, Kalvan and I were off to the airport and winging our way home in fair skies. We had some change in scenery on the return trip and made a point of flying over Monument Valley. I love to pick out all the monuments that I can name but, in particular, the Totem (as seen in the *Eiger Sanction* with Clint Eastwood). It was a long flight through the Four Corners region, but I never bore of it.

Again, more midday thermals and a taxing hot wind prolonged our journey. We made it to Winslow, Arizona, for fuel and to stretch our legs. From there on, it was our "backyard." We overflew Jack's Canyon, where I have made many weekend climbing outings. Near Payson, we saw angry columns of white smoke whipped by the uplifted scalding air. The water in natural vegetation evaporates and forms steam. In turn, this colors the smoke white, and the rising air potentiates the wild fire, drawing in fresh air to fuel the flames. Back at the Deer Valley Airport, I parked the Cessna, and we each headed to our respective homes. It had been a great trip, and I felt like I had pushed my vertical limits.

CHAPTER TWO
Flight of the Phoenix
or The Year of Living Dangerously

We planned on a big wall climb, and the Zion weather was forecast to be good. I wasn't crazy about sandstone, but Kalvan had his head in the clouds and his sights set on Spaceshot. We read all the guidebooks, organized gear, and reserved a car at the St. George Utah Airport. It was an uneventful flight in the Cessna 172 to the sleepy town and an easy traverse across the lower wild and scenic Grand Canyon. The car was a black Dodge Charger; we loaded it and were headed to Zion National Park in no time. Silently I fantasized about the '68 Ford Mustang and Dodge Charger car chase in the movie *Bullitt*. Oh yeah, but the guys in the Charger died in a ball of fire; maybe that wasn't such a good plan.

In our Springdale motel room, we freshened up and proceeded to the local climbing store to check out their equipment selection. I bought approach shoes, and Kalvan purchased a new lead rope. After a leisurely dinner, we selected our gear, loaded backpacks, and laid out clothes for an alpine start. We went to bed early to catch the 6:30 a.m. Zion Canyon Shuttle departure into the park from the south entrance.

As we entered Zion with eager eyes in the early morning light, red sandstone walls hovered around us, reaching to the sky. Some towered 3,000 feet into the air. In the dark, deep canyon with vividly colored steep walls, my gaze shot back and forth from one fantastic view to another. The striated convoluted walls burst with an extraordinary range of wonderfully soft pastel light.

> There is an eloquence to their forms which stirs the imagination with a singular power and kindles in the mind . . . a glowing response . . . . Nothing can exceed the wondrous beauty of Zion . . . in the nobility and beauty of the sculptures there is no comparison.

These words were penned by Clarence E. Dutton, a pioneer geologist in 1880.

A short bus ride led us literally to the base of the climb. An easy scramble put us in the area where we were to rope up. No longer the tourist, I lead the start off with a funky 5.6, followed by a 5.7, a typically awkward sandstone pitch for me. Next, a 5.5 ended in an area just below a small party on a two-level port-a-ledge. They were friendly but had not been awake that long; at least one climber was still in her sleeping bag. Immediately, pitch 4 started with A1 (read that, bolt ladder). Kalvan led it. I jugged it, and Kalvan hoisted the pack on our haul line. We would repeat this routine for most of the rest of the ascent. Off to a confident start, the next couple of pitches were stiff (5.11+) but uneventful. Kalvan made it look easy and maintained a good pace!

The sandstone rock and crack were good quality, and the steep wall mostly vertical and smooth, with occasional relief enough for a purchase with one foot in the crack and the other smeared on the face. Each move was calculated and solid protection "pro" placed at frequent intervals in the plum fissure. Fingers and hands were the key to any movement up the route. Both nuts and cams were used interchangeably in the meandering fracture. The crack ranged in size from fingertips to thin hands to bomber hands.

Randy Lippincott on Spaceshot with the Virgin River in the background.
Photo by Kalvan Swanky.

I followed and cleaned the pitch as I jumared up the vertical sandstone. Now, eight hundred feet off the valley floor, I looked down at the tiny ribbon of highway, the Virgin River, and a passing bus like the one that brought us into the park. Unexpectedly I was no longer just an observer; I had become part of the scenic phenomenon in Zion. Now the people in the bus were looking up at us on the giant sandstone wall! The distant river clamored with subdued optimism in the background. Suddenly my chest stiffened, my pupils dilated, and my hands tightly gripped the jumars; I thought, *So this is what a big wall is like.* I took a long breath, slowly exhaled, and refocused on my duties.

The Incredible Hulk

I would climb other big faces in my future but in much more remote areas. The Hulk was as demanding as it was distant. My waist was on fire. I had been leaning back in my harness in a forced awkward stance too long. Suddenly I had to divert my attention from Matt Peres to my immediate situation. I grabbed at the multiple colored slings in front of me from my airy perch and pulled myself into the cold rock as I arched my lumbar region. I had to redirect the pressure onto my leg loops. Warm blood rushed into the small of my back, and it began to tingle. Momentarily the world was right again. I repeated this maneuver several times during the remainder of the pitch and was happy to begin climbing when Matt started to belay me. One third of the way up the 1,500-foot face, I embraced the primordial defect in the rock for which the climb was named; it was me and the granite again. Mano a mano, I could handle this. I knew I could power my way up the Red Dihedral; for me, it was a pure struggle with gravity and stone, and I was more determined!

Matt Peres leading on the Red Dihedral pitch, the Incredible Hulk.
"This is longer than it looks." Photo by Randy Lippincott.

It was the fourth pitch on the Red Dihedral and, for me, the
heart of our objective. As soon as Matt started out, he turned to me
and said, "This is longer than it looks." I recalled from the guidebook,
"This is one of those peaks that is much larger than it looks. From
the base and approach, the upper pitches are not visible so when you
are on the climb it keeps going and going and going." Immediately
I was happy that we were not running the last pitch and this one
together with the seventy-meter rope. Issues would have been rope
drag and endurance but, most of all, the ability to see each other and
communicate while on the route. Matt and I had discussed nonverbal
communication prior to starting the climb. To be isolated from your
partner can add to the intimidation of the climb, and I needed Matt's
support. Due to the possibility of high winds on the rock face, we
required a way to clearly communicate to avoid any potential for

catastrophic or fatal mistakes. We did not need this random factor to complicate our already-tenuous situation.

To start a pitch (a rope length or section of climb to be done in one continuous lead), the leader (the person going first) and the belayer (the person playing out rope through a brake device) are in direct proximity to each other. As the leader reaches the end of that section to be climbed (a pitch), he may not be visible to the belayer, and it may be impossible to hear him because of the wind or other factors. The agreement was until such time that the leader signals orally or with five distinct long rope pulls, alternating with exaggerated slack, he would remain on belay (tied to the other person with a dynamically taut rope). The above procedure indicated he had secured three anchors at the next belay stance and could be safely taken off belay from below.

The procedure gave me time to dismantle my belay station and prepare to climb as soon as all the slack was taken from the rope. The number-two person removes the pro (short for protection, nuts or mechanical devices placed in the rock to "catch" or minimize the distance the leader may potentially fall). The second cleans the route as he climbs so we do not deface the rock or leave anything to show we were ever there (therefore the term *clean climbing*).

Time is safety in the alpine setting, both from a weather and light-of-day standpoint. We needed to move in a flowing and synchronous fashion to gain the summit and descend during the daylight hours. The fall weather did not threaten us with a midday thunderstorm but, rather, the attenuated daylight. Down climbing or descending an unfamiliar route in the dark is inherently time-consuming and dangerous. Over the years these have always been my most anxious moments.

During the first three pitches, I had to check my progress as the rope was well below me after several moves, so I would stop to allow Matt to reel it in. Eventually I did communicate this to Matt—that in fact, I could climb faster if he took in the rope faster. It worked for both of us.

Now, indeed, it was my turn to embrace the Red Dihedral. Admittedly I don't do well in cracks, and this was a long and serious crack. I learned to climb on faces in Utah using smearing and crimping techniques on flakes and ledges. I had trained in the gym for this crack, but it was a pitiful exercise. I used gloves that fit over my meticulously taped hands to keep warm while belaying, but the gloves came off for my communion with the rock. It did help after the first pitch, as my hands were numb from the cold hard granite. I was hopeful that it would warm up during the day.

Now, in the Red Dihedral, I was alternating between bomber hand jams and dreaded tenuous finger locks. My left foot performed like it was on black ice; it was nearly useless. My hands were simple tools and seemed impervious to the temperature of the rock now. It was as if I were a novice, yearning for my next good fist jam like a pathetic junkie. A fix that would only last a few minutes at best, only until I could step up and throw a knuckle sandwich at the Hulk's midsection! And then I just needed my next "shot."

Randy Lippincott on the third pitch of the Red Dihedral,
the Incredible Hulk. Photo by Matt Peres.

Oh please, let it be closer than it looks, just enough to eke out a few more feet to reach the next piece of pro. A struggle, a pump fest at the very best, a desperate scuffle with a predestined equation: the force required for upward movement is the difference between the cubed volume of the void in the rock times the inverse of the linear gravity squared. *And* did I adjust for the angle of the dangle? *What*—I was so screwed! I had bitten off more than I could chew. But I was working through it. One foot at a time, one move at a time, I was making headway. Sweating—yes, huffing—yes, straining—yes, moving up—*yes!* This was the very soul of the climb. I could only look up. I could not bear to look down past my feet; that would be negative energy. That alone could tip the scales. I had to focus. I must do everything to maintain my upward momentum. If I did not continue to move with the rope, we would be forced to bivouac into the frigid night, huddled inside our respective thin backpacks with no food, fuel, additional insulation, and little water.

My hands were meticulously taped to guard against abrasion and manageable for the assault, but it was my feet that were not meeting the challenge. My left foot was on polished granite, and that completely distracted my right foot from even participating in the struggle. I needed to strategically place my hands in the crack and stem with my legs, smearing my feet as an opposing triad. The more extremities that I could involve in the struggle, the less force was applied on each one. My right foot should be used in the crack when able to relieve the strain on my hands. So single-mindedly, I forgot the basics and stressed until I was breathing too hard, actually panting, I had to stop and rest. *"Take!"* I yelled. This was the rescue signal for Matt to fix the rope so I could hang on him and relax and recover my strength and composure in the dihedral. I was nearing hyperventilation. I had to shake my arms below my waist and allow blood to return to my fingers, forearms, and brain. During the first pitch, Matt had remarked how wonderfully sticky his climbing shoes felt. In my geosphere, all of that had just simply vanished for me.

As if I didn't already know my climbing was in question, my left long and index finger suddenly and unexpectedly locked! Oh no, I had seen this happen, but it was in a depleted electrolyte situation when my partner had been sweating out more than his sodium and potassium intake. This was not the case today. I had to use my right hand to straighten out the fingers on my left hand; it was so mechanically painful. As if on cue, next my right hand started to spasm and go into tetany (the protracted, involuntary mechanical flexion of the digit, a one-way sustained focal muscle convulsion). My long and ring finger on my right hand followed suit. They spasmed; the forearm muscle cramped and locked in flexion.

This time I had to force them into extension with my mouth. The knot in my forearm would spontaneously recur. This happened repeatedly until the end of the pitch. I felt like the knotted snake in a *Far Side* cartoon. I was worried and mentally was ready to bail from a most practical standpoint. I wanted to rap the face, return to camp, and lie in my warm sleeping bag looking up at the blue sky, breathing deeply, in peaceful meditation. I wanted to descend because I felt I could no longer perform my duties safely. My struggle was both physical and mental.

The more difficult 5.10b exit from the Red Dihedral was, in fact, a welcome combination for me, a nonevent. This was incongruent to any observer as the hand crack was only rated 5.9. I had to get my mind right; maybe I just wasn't paying attention. As I stemmed out of the dihedral into sunshine, there was Matt waiting for me. It had to be easier ahead of us. I was confident, I was relieved, and I just wanted to get on with the next pitch. There was less wind, and we were in direct sunlight now. It was warmer, and everything seemed better. It was also well after 1:00 p.m. Four hours into the climb and daylight now was a real factor—it had started to dwindle! Where had the time gone?

At the end of the pitch, I expressed my concerns to Matt, but he reasoned it was better to go on and that this was not the place to rappel. After pitch 4, my body was graced with open-handed holds and, ultimately, flushed the lactic acid that had built up and caused the clawlike forearm distortions. I was so thankful to regain the full function of my hands! Again I could climb and belay with confidence! In fact, I knew I was consuming enough water and electrolytes.

From this vantage point, we could see Kalvan and Sarah on Positive Vibrations to the climbers left, a sheer, impressively exposed blank face. My camera came out for the compulsory photos. It would be striking from any angle, but it looked truly imposing from this perspective. We were only slightly above them at this point. The entire face of the Incredible Hulk was awesome; it was vertical, it was clean, it was foreboding, it was impossible! I watched Kalvan lead. Over the short period of time, I saw him fall twice, both with a resounding "Shit!" I don't think in seven years of climbing together I had ever heard Kalvan swear on lead before. I guess it was some really difficult climbing or that maybe he was off route. It was my turn to head out before Sarah started, so I did not watch her move across the face. Even for that short time, from that distance, it was comforting to know there were other climbers in our proximity. For in this wilderness situation, miscalculations may quickly compound themselves.

Although we waited until 9:00 a.m. to begin climbing, at the end of the first pitch, my fingers were cold and numb. We would not move into sunshine until afternoon, and frankly, I was a bit worried. I knew from years of outdoors activity how quickly the rock could sap the warmth from your digits. I wore gloves at the belay stance and quickly warmed my fingers even with minimal activity. My climbing was not yet in question, but I did experience an old phenomenon, "sewing-machine legs." It actually was only my upwind leg that began to shake and quiver uncontrollably. My singular leg bounced rhythmically on my toe. I was cold, it was windy, and my leg muscles were irritable from the strenuous hike to base camp. I did not feel uncontrollable fear. It was not the altitude. So the right leg's objective was to warm me at the belay stance, with or without my consent.

I recalled a similar scenario forty-four years prior. The sixteenth of March 1969, over Agnew, Nebraska, in a Cessna 182 with the right door removed for skydiving. It was my first parachute jump. I was excited, and there was a lot of empty space filled with gravity between my boots and terra firma. The frigid air blast was focused on my leg as I sat on my butt, exposed to the frigid elements, waiting to exit the aircraft. Then as now, as I contemplated my position, my leg trembled uncontrollably, waiting for what was to come next. I remembered a favorite quote of mine, "I get stronger when I shake" (John Yablonski).

The idea for the Hulk began in May 2011. Kalvan had a connection in Durango, Kurt Blair and Aaron Robinson. They hopped a flight through Denver to Phoenix. Kalvan picked them up at Skyharbor while I prepared the Columbia 400 for a direct flight to Mammoth, California. The weather alternate was the Red Rocks area, west of Las Vegas. Late season heavy snow in the Sierras diverted us to Henderson Field in Las Vegas and the Red Rocks Casino. It was three of my best days of really fun climbing. Kalvan and I started with the super sketchy and pumpy climb, Risky Business. Ultimately we climbed Prince of Darkness in Black Velvet Canyon. However, the coup de grâce was when all four of us made the sweet discovery of Crimson Chrysalis. It was truly a remarkable clean and varied nine-pitch climb. Once we "summited," we all wanted to turn around and do it all over again; it really was that great. And we didn't have to share it with anyone.

Since that time, Kalvan had kept the Hulk and Positive Vibrations at the top of his tick list. This time, his connections through work matched us with Matt Peres and Sarah Malone. I was skeptical; how could we be introduced to nicer, more talented people than Kurt and Aaron? The chances were slim, but what could I do but go along with the program? The date was set. I e-mailed twenty-eight-year-old Matt regarding my level of commitment and ability—admittedly, I did not mention that I was drawing social security.

Kalvan arranged the flight to Reno, where we were planning to meet Matt and Sarah at baggage claim Thursday evening. Sarah had previously arranged for a killer deal on a "midsized" car. Everyone had two bags, and they filled every available square inch of that automobile. Yeah, *road trip!* But first it was off to the El Dorado where the rooms were advertised at thirty-five dollars a night. When Kalvan came back from the desk, he had his poker face on and explained the rooms were not thirty-five dollars but, rather, twenty-nine dollars—*ca ching!* Let's eat. It allowed us to visit, get to know each other, plan the travel-and-approach day, and go to bed early. We met downstairs for breakfast the next morning and were on the road in no time after a stop at Walmart for white gas and Crown Royal.

At the Bridgeport Ranger Station, we listened to the dos and don'ts and received our back-country permit for the Hulk base camp. At Twin Lakes, we sorted gear, parked the car, and donned packs. Sarah needed help getting hers on and, before the end of the trip, swore she would never carry such a heavy load again. Been there, done that, got the T-shirt!

The trek in was pleasant and scenic until we crossed crystal-clear Robinson Creek and immediately started our steep ascent up Little Slide Canyon. There was some trail, some snowfields, and lots of boulders to hop with a heavy pack on your back. This maze seemed endless until we came to our campsite with a spectacular view of the Incredible Hulk directly in front of us. Indeed it was sublimely grand, and we shared it with no one. We laid out sleeping bags; I assembled my stove while Sarah erected her tent. Then we were graced with a hot spicy meal, alpenglow, and spectacular red skies laced with scattered lenticular clouds through the failing light. The barometer was holding steady, and the weather forecast was good.

A Crown Royal snow cone for desert set the scene for some camp stories as we crowded together into Sarah's homey tent. I was forced to relate some of my army adventures. Since Sarah is a veterinarian, Kalvan insisted I tell the "The Tale of Sue," my beagle patient in Special Forces dog lab. Yes, back then, SF used dogs from the pound to practice battlefield surgery on. Soon Sarah tired of us, and it was bivy time. Once outdoors, we were witness to a *real big* portion of sky that was on loan from Montana. I don't recall a more vivid Milky Way or brighter stars since I was a kid on the farm. The near-full moonrise at 11:40 p.m. was no exception. Matt and I both had to cover our eyes to shut out the incredibly bright moonlight. Maybe the new go-to refreshment, Crown Royal, really did have some connection with the moonshine.

In the morning it was more of the same. What a spectacular place; what an awesome setting. It was pre-Jurassic but without the velociraptors. At 7:30 a.m., it seemed more prudent to be in my sleeping bag than bang my fingers into the ice-cold hard rock. After all, we did sleep next to a very large snowfield. Following dinner, I filled my insulated Nalgene bottle with boiling water and used it as a hot-water bottle in my sleeping bag; it was fabulous. I used the now-warm water in the morning to quickly boil it for coffee and oatmeal. The morning light was encouraging, but the temperature was not that inviting. The rest of the day, our calories would come out of our pockets. I supplied Matt with liquid high-energy squeeze tubes and Trio bars for lunch. We both had three-liter Gatorade-augmented hydration systems in our packs along with shoes, headlamps, and an extra jacket.

I filled my one-liter MSR fuel bottle with white gas for the stove. Sarah left her canister stove at the car to lighten her already-bulging load unbeknownst to me. All we had was one heat source for the four of us. The first night it was windy, and we burned the MSR XGK stove continuously for well over 3 hours at 9,000 feet. We were all disappointed to discover the next morning that only about two inches of fuel remained in the one-liter bottle. That jaded our decision making the following day. No one really wanted to stay without adequate fuel for the four of us. The only things that I could have done differently were boil stream water instead of melting snow and cook in the tent. I'm sure this would have nearly doubled our effective BTUs.

After the late breakfast, Matt and I geared up and approached the Hulk across the snowfield and scree slope in monastic reverence. According to the guidebook, "the Incredible Hulk is known for three things: the best rock in the high Sierra, long routes, and incredibly sustained climbing. There are no easy routes on this face and unlike most Sierra climbs, The Incredible Hulk remains sustained and challenging for the majority of the pitches. The rock is clean and relatively unfractured and is more reminiscent of Yosemite climbing than the typical high Sierra peak." We found the guidebook accurate: "The first half of the climb is sustained and follows major crack systems. The second half ascends more broken rock on easier terrain with the occasional 5.8 or 5.9 sections." Above pitch 4, the nitty-gritty section, route finding was somewhat more difficult. There are variations for the upper sections, but when in doubt, we climbed straight up. This seemed to work well for us as our progress was smooth and continuous.

Now my hands and feet were both working well. There was the occasional gust of wind, but the sky was not threatening. Our communication and rope management was good. I noted the time and wished I had not been so cavalier when it came to getting out of my sleeping bag. I wanted to watch Kalvan and Sarah climb, but there was no timetable for that, and anyhow we were on the far side of the arête, out of view. In due fashion, Matt and I powwowed at the top of the tenth pitch; we hurriedly reviewed our map of the route and decided to look for the rap station into the dangerous and icy north couloir. Why bother with the last two very easy pitches and the known single rap? I was still somewhat confused, but in an instant, we were committed to plan B.

The descent . . . The guidebook words were burned in the back of my mind: "Move fast. Descending from the summit (specifically, finding the rappel) is difficult and dangerous in the dark." We were close to pushing that envelope. At best, I figured we had sixty minutes of daylight. I configured my headlamp on my helmet and prayed for anchors. OK, admittedly I *did not* have a clear picture of our retreat following the tenth pitch. My vote was to exit and start home ASAP, but which way—north couloir or south couloir? The map was specific: "Walk southeast for 200 feet on 3rd class (rock), escape to the *southwest* notch—requires rappels and down climbing." Weren't those mutually exclusive events? Logically the southern exposure should be free of snow and ice.

We were headed to the north gully, *not* the south! OK, what I was looking at was a friggin' big snowbank; that was not indicated on the map. I was in my skinny, slippery, smooth climbing shoes. To mount those icy slopes in this gear was tenuous at best. Yes, I was getting "cold feet." I could see myself taking a ride on the icy slope and being ejected into space. I'm nearly positive the free fall would have been less than—oh say, maybe *ten* seconds. You know, a falling body accelerates at 32.1522 feet per second squared; it looked to be 1,000 feet to the couloir below. The narrow canyon walls looked steep and unforgiving. Our shouted communication mockingly echoed off them.

I belayed Matt on tension to a cryptic spot for the rappel. A single rusty piton marked the location. Were there no slings on it because it had been used to climb up, or had someone actually pulled a rope through the piton without using a carabineer? It didn't look like it had been used for a very, very long time, but we took it—hook, line, and piton. We backed up the pin, burned gear including two biners, and rapped into the abyss. Matt stopped on a ledge, and I followed suit. We built our own rappel station because we found no gear or indication that we were on the right path, only that we were headed down. When Matt was set to push off on the second rappel, I looked him in the eyes and said, "Good luck." Apparently it worked; in only a minute, I had confirmation of a rappel station. Yes, our situation started to look brighter! Our luck had changed! Another setup, another double-rope rappel, but this time when we pulled the rope in a routine maneuver, it stuck behind a large imposing flake high above us. Oh no, this did not look good. Daylight was fading fast. This was getting complicated and worrisome. Matt coolly tied in as I belayed him up the 20 feet to free the jammed rope. It took less than five minutes, and we were back in business!

The rope was bicolored so we could easily find the middle to set up the rappel. I was busy pulling the rope as Matt backed up the next anchor. Just prior to whipping the rope off the station, I looked over at Matt to confirm that he had secured the rope with a carabineer. *It was not!* My heart sank! If I had truly been in a hurry, both ends of our lifeline would have gone over the edge, leaving us stranded on the dark side of the Hulk halfway down the great wall! I paused and took a deep breath and composed myself. After I verified that it, in fact, was secured to the anchor, I pulled the rope and tied a knot in the other end, just as we had done for each rappel.

Five rappels got us to the ice and snow-choked broad gully. Three more expeditious rappels got us around several nunataks off the ice and onto dry rock. At that point, we changed into our approach shoes. We found that ambient light was enough for us to safely find our way back to base camp through the extremely long scree field. At that point boulder hopping was anticlimactic. It was 7:00 p.m. and Crown Royal never sounded so good. Matt had won the day with his cool head and leading skill. We made a good team and did it in a safe fashion. That meant a lot to me.

After our return to Scottsdale, I had a conversation at the local climbing gym with Tim, who had just climbed the Red Dihedral in August. He told me that it would have been safer and faster to finish the last two easy pitches and exit to the southeast. From the summit, a short down climb to a well-used rappel station and an easy forty-five minutes to the base of the climb and then camp. Part of that may have been correct, but we couldn't know just how much snow we would have had to navigate on the down climb. The risk of the multiple dicey rappels into the north gully still looms large in my memory. That was a setup for the classic climbing accident: end of the day and tired, lowered defenses, dwindling light, in somewhat of a hurry, and completely dependent on a single-use anchor system. For the climber, the rappel is a blasé and risky but necessary evil.

We elected to conserve fuel and go all out for breakfast. I guess I don't remember any real dinner, just snacking and hydrating, and it was time for the ol' fart sack. Although I thought that I had dressed warmer, I was chilly throughout the night. The moon rose fifty minutes later than the day before in a clear sky, but I was prepared to shield my eyes from the penetrating light with my bandanna. I was restless; I had some leg cramping and carpal tunnel syndrome symptoms in both hands depending on how they were positioned within the tight three-season bag. I welcomed daybreak and filled the cook pot with water and cranked up the stove. In a short time, we were sipping coffee and had our quota of oatmeal. Sarah elected not to participate in a hot breakfast.

It was going to be another perfect day. I was ready to head out. My spirits were high, but my fingers were tender, triceps painful, and calves sore. The steep descent was arduous at best—lots of boulder hopping, jumping, and high stepping with full packs. All of us were sorry to see Sarah carry such a large, awkward pack, but she was a trooper. Matt twisted both ankles at some point, but it was not serious.

Back in Twin Lakes, we stopped for the famous burgers. After sitting for the eagerly awaited meal, we looked like zombies walking stiff legged when we got up from the table. We repacked the car and headed back to Reno. Matt and Sarah bid us farewell at the airport, and Kalvan and I hopped a southwest flight home.

Chapter Two: Spaceshot (cont'd)

That morning in Zion Park, the only thing that I was really in control of was my mind. I had learned early in the climbing game that 50 percent of the task was brain control. If you think you are going to fall, you set yourself up for failure. That must never divert your concentration on what's at hand. Reality is secondary to your duty and commitment to your task. I must be "in the zone" or go home. I flashed back on a Lobo, saying, "Finger locks or pine box."

Very early (about 10:00 a.m.), pitch 5 brought us into the sun, and in no time, we could feel its harsh effects on the rocky face and our bodies. At first I could ignore the rays. Then I found myself rolling my sleeves down for sun protection. Next I added a bandanna to my neck in addition to my helmet. Initially the sandstone seemed friendly, soft, and smooth in a pleasing pastel rose iron red. Once baking was well underway, the gritty stone seemed to find its way into my shirt, shoes, and mouth. It was powered only by gravity as there was not a breath of wind anywhere except on rare occasion. The intermittent breeze teased me with what I was so desperately missing. The granular "single-cell red comets" were in search of the source of gravity. They accelerated until impacting a horizontal surface. Then the individual grains rested until the wind engaged them in a dance of saltation. They were light enough not to be heard but united enough to form the Sahara Desert. Like all rock, this sandstone was in a state of entropy; however, in geologic time, this abutment was in a big hurry.

Kalvan Swanky leading on Spaceshot, Zion Park, Utah.
Photo by Randy Lippincott.

The white hot light found its way behind my sunglasses, and my neck and eyes became sore from straining, looking up, and squinting. I positioned my body to shade my feet as they cooked on contact with the roasting rock. Time seemed to stand still, but our water was quickly running short. Sweat attracted the grit and made an extremely bothersome abrasive paste between my fingers. My biceps hinted at fatigue, but my thighs and legs seemed to repeat a flexion/extension exercise on a marathon scale. I had cottonmouth after each sprint up the route. In a short time, I gained a rhythm on the rope with the jumars. It was a fine line between efficiency and conservation. It was baptism by fire, and my mind was being tempered by the same flame as my body.

Kalvan made good progress in the crack until the end of the fifth pitch. The sun no longer produced any contrasting shade on the face to accentuate the slightest relief in the varnished rock to aid with our route-finding ability. In the intense full light, the stone seemed flat and our course on it difficult to discern. In the severe sunlight, it was tricky to find the zigzag of the route—where one crack ended and transitioned to another one parallel to it.

I knew Kalvan had been drinking enough early on when I saw a dark fluid serpent on the rock originate from his position and end fifteen feet below him. As I reached his hanging belay stance, we shared the last of our water. It was 10:00 a.m. Somehow we didn't account for the calm air, intense heat, and extreme labor to scale the heat-soaked face.

Now that we had settled into a pattern, we paced ourselves with pitch 6 and 7. We conserved both energy and our sweat. There would be no shortcuts on this climb, and we were in it for the duration. In fact, we had reached the ubiquitous point of no return. We had moved beyond any possible exit strategy for us. Due to the right leaning arch we were climbing, any rappel at this point would lead off into space. Unable to contact the rock when I would have reached the end of the rope, it would make *any* retreat impossible. The only movement for consideration was upward. Like the movie, *Flight of the Phoenix*, if we didn't rise from the ashes, we wouldn't be going home.

The route follows the left side of the arch and reveals the impossibility of retreat once more than half way up. Photo by Randy Lippincott.

The heat was irrepressible. The still air scorched the pursed lips when inhaled decisively. Slowly but surely the high temperature was sapping my strength. I could feel time start to slow. It was more than uncomfortable; the heat was hijacking my endurance. I looked at the river far below with contempt. The source of my relief was so close yet so impossibly far away. Bathed in the oppressive, inescapable oven, I could only accept my position and try to pace my struggles. I had broken a sweat with my strenuous efforts in my attempt to maintain the pace and our schedule. The sun and heat irritated my exposed skin. When I paused between pitches, I refocused on myself; formication was an overbearing distraction. My arms and legs had been overheated, baked in the sun, overworked; they were irritable, twitchy, prickly, and it felt like waves of tiny insects were crawling under my skin. It was distracting.

At the completion of the seventh sunny pitch, we arrived at Earth Orbit Ledge. This was a small but very comfortable outcrop where we stopped for a breather (our first real break of the day) and pictures. Kalvan took off his shoes to dissipate some heat and remove any "hitchhikers." He dumped out enough sand to operate a medium-sized egg timer. We both had a power bar and looked at the hydration bottle, wishing for a drink of water.

The food sat in my mouth until I generated enough moisture to swallow; it was almost impossible. With each additional bite, I was able to muster less and less saliva. I was losing interest fast. If only I had some gum to chew, it might not seem so bad. I think fatigue was starting to set in. With dehydration, strength is the first to go, and judgment soon to follow. Recently at an Arizona National Park, I noticed a sign as I left the visitor center. It read, "Feeling cranky? Irritability, headaches, dizziness, and fatigue are all signs of dehydration. Always carry water with you on the trail. If you're thirsty now, it means that your body is already dehydrated." I didn't have any time to be cranky; I had to be focused.

The lead off Earth Orbit Ledge was indeed a distraction and a needed injection of adrenalin. It was awkward and committing to reach the short crack; the move was stout, and the view was airy. Now my struggle came down to this, the top of the climb was not just several hundred feet or hours to the finish. The stubborn crack was scarcely beyond my reach but, rather, a whole world away. To look down was more than 1,000 feet of free space in the apex of the colossal sandstone arch. Then very abruptly, some intimidating huge red rocks blocked any kind of welcomed reception. Now, it was more like 97 percent mental. My clouds of doubt did nothing to mitigate the intense rays of the sun. I knew what had to be done.

Yes, I can do this, it will probably be OK. I'm sure the rope will hold (although it really feels a lot smaller than when we started). If I fall, it will not hurt and not really last that long. It should be quick! The surreal line between the twilight zone and reality was smeared. *OK, now focus on what's at hand. Climb, move, and think what to do next. Most of all, control the fear. Bring the gear, carry the now-empty pack, endeavor not to strain, and try to pace yourself, economize your moves,* I told myself. If I tore a fingernail free of its bed, split my knuckle, rubbed a blister raw, the question was not if it was painful but, rather, if I minded—it quite simply no longer mattered. First things first. I had to take care of business.

It was evident that now the sun was low in the sky. Without hurrying, we had to pick up the pace for two reasons. First, it would be easier and safer to find our way down in the daylight (yes, we did have our headlamps with us), and second, the last bus departed at 9:00 p.m. We didn't want the double jeopardy of being late and having to walk the ten miles back to town in the middle of the night. I had already accepted the fact that it was going to be a very long, dry moonlit stroll back to our room. Certainly the restaurants would be closed by then.

I used aid to turn the corner at the zenith of the arch, but the difficulty quickly eased off. It was the most exposed view I have ever had the privilege of experiencing while rock climbing. The 200-foot rope dangling free in the air looked like spaghetti off the end of my fork. My very own insignificance was nearly immobilizing. I savored my inaction to indelibly imprint this moment in my memory for all time. It was not unlike my first skydive—all air and mind control, minus the parachute. Although I fully realized my position, it was as if I were a neutral observer of a scientific experiment. I was unattached, aloof to the potential consequences but did realize I had no reserve parachute. It was beautiful, humbling, and overwhelming; if I survived this, it was going in my top five climb list!

Island in the Sky

Mount Hayes in 1986 was the most aesthetic Alaskan climb that I had done and is also on my all-time top-five list. It instilled wilderness big-mountain logistics and excitement in a classic expedition. We chartered Tamarack Air to fly us to the West Fork of the Trident Glacier in the Alaska Range. Chief pilot Kem Sibbert was familiar with the safe landing zones and equally aware of the objective dangers of crevasses and icefall on the glacier. After loading the voluminous gear in the ski-equipped Cessna 185, we bid our farewells. Although I had taken two weeks off and carried three weeks of food, we hoped to do the climb in one week. The latest report of snow conditions in the Hayes group was excellent. Minimal avalanche danger, closed crevasses, and hardpack snow for easy trekking. This was all great news.

Blessed with exceptional weather, we landed within three miles of the base of our objective on the glacier. Already in the shadow of the mountain, we quickly set up camp and discussed plans for the next day. The scenery was breathtaking and vistas on a par with any in the Alaska Range, to include McKinley. Within the first hour, I witnessed the most spectacular natural phenomenon that I have ever observed up close. From approximately 5,000 feet above the valley floor, a nearby mountain released thousands of tons of emerald-green glacier ice. Starting with as much force as a Midwestern thunderstorm, the ice continued to roar downward, increasing in speed and volume as it was pulverized during its metamorphosis and self-destruction. I watched the billowing white mass consume the valley floor and continue unobstructed an additional half mile, horizontally forcing clouds of snow 2,000 feet into the air. In a word, awesome! Beautiful to observe from afar, majestic, but deadly if caught in the devouring path.

I remembered my visit with Carl Tobin during his hospitalization in September 1984 at Fairbanks Memorial Hospital. He was recovering from surgery after he had suffered two broken legs in an avalanche not far from where I stood. I was impressed by his positive attitude and the fact that he was already starting his own rehabilitation the day of surgery. Later he described the incident:

> When the slab cut loose, my mind calculated trajectories, analyzed terrain, and fed me its conclusions: no way out, you are going to die. This conclusion seemed to free me to experience the fall. Tumbling, catching air, then the loudest sound I've ever heard—probably the sound of both legs breaking or how to get hit by a Mack truck.

Yes, I could relate to this helpless feeling and the Mack truck, as though you are only an observer and, in fact, have no control of what is about to happen. Your only guarantee is to be the first one to the scene of the accident.

My insignificance in nature was reconfirmed. Size and distance tend to fool you in this wide-open wild country. Coined the Alaska factor, what looks like 2,000 feet is over a mile. What should take a few days may take weeks. Anything that is too big, too far, too cold, or too difficult can be explained by the *Alaska factor*.

During the next eight days, I was privileged to witness more than fifty similar spontaneous ice and snow avalanches. The grand finale occurred on the day of our departure. The east face of Mount Hayes released an unrivaled ice avalanche from the summit ice field, nearly the expanse of its 7,000-foot vertical face. The brunt of the inconceivable force was deflected latterly, but at over two miles away, we still received fallout from the eruption. A spellbinding Hiroshima-sized release of kinetic energy that overloaded both the optic and auditory senses. For me this was a once-in-a-lifetime event to savor and reminisce about. It was on scale with a tornado, volcano, hurricane, or tidal wave and just as deadly. I could relate to the tourist standing on the beach mesmerized, watching the water withdraw from the shore just prior to the tsunami.

Spontaneous hanging glacier avalanche, full length of the
7,000-foot east face of Mount Hayes. Photo by Randy Lippincott.

The climbing party included me as senior member and American Alpine Club representative Randy McGregor, an anesthesiologist from Fairbanks, Alaska, and Martin Leonard III, body builder and elementary teacher from Buckland, Alaska. We were roped together on the glacier for safety although crevasse danger in this area was minimal. At the end of the first full day, we camped at a point where the head of the Trident glacier met the 3,000-foot ramp joining the east ridge of Mount Hayes. The top of this steep ramp was named Levi's Bump by the East Ridge first-ascent party in 1972. Although the ramp appeared safe enough, little did we know how long and strenuous the approach would be. The true first ascent of Mount Hayes was by the famous Bradford Washburn via the serpentine North Ridge in 1941.

In deteriorating weather the third day, we elected to take only the climbing essentials and food for eight days. We carried expanded packs of eighty pounds; the easy ramp became a death march. Near the top section of the route, we were further encumbered by intermittent whiteouts. Guarded by a rock buttress on either side, a narrow, steep snowfield led to Levi's Bump; the area was coined the Portal. Our choices at that point included (1) open bivouac, (2) cache our gear and descend to our lower camp, or (3) push on in marginal conditions. I felt Levi's Bump was within our grasp, wanted to continue moving upward, and volunteered to establish the route without my pack.

I placed small wands—3-foot-long green garden bamboo shafts with red flags on top—at ten-yard intervals to mark my route; unprotected I climbed upward. As the storm's tempo increased, I was halted for five to ten minutes at a time shielding my face from the bite of the icy wind and horizontal stinging snow, unable to see or move. At last, on hands and knees, I found myself on a 30 × 100 foot level area. As I peered through the white fury, I was unable to distinguish cornice from abyss. Eventually I convinced myself that I was at my destination, that I was, in fact, on Levi's bump. After painfully marking the boundary of the small "summit" in the whiteout conditions, I retraced my well-marked path to the Portal.

When I described our proximity to our intermediate goal, we decided to push on through the tempest. With all available rope, again I climbed ahead and secured nearly 900 feet so the "bump" could be safely assaulted in the deteriorating conditions. McGregor and Leonard used jumars attached to the rope to safely guide them through the storm with their heavy loads. Alone I retraced my steps for the third time, retrieving my heavy pack. My return was greeted by an erected tent on the secured "bump" and hot soup, the first course in a hard-earned meal. One by one, we drifted off to sleep with satisfied appetites and aching backs. Foggy minds reluctantly were startled to reality by the thunder of nearby avalanches, only to slip back into unconsciousness. The tent walls flexed rhythmically in the wind as it provided a radiant cocoon of comfort for the exhausted travelers. Levi's Bump had chalked up another one for the Alaska Factor.

Fourteen hours in a sleeping bag did not completely refresh us, but the midmorning sun seemed to be focused on our "island in the sky." At 9,750 feet, our high camp was literally at the base of the East Ridge. Our extraordinary view was unrestricted; it drew us toward the glorious sight and uplifted our spirits. The monotonous white sculptured stairway beckoned toward the summit like a siren. Able to see the entire route close-up, we mentally toyed with individual strategies. Although our tent had survived the storm, we were painfully aware of the weather those mountains could produce. A snow cave was the order of the day! After assessing prevailing winds and snow conditions, a site was chosen, and work commenced. Drying gear in the sun and restoring one's nutritional status were first on the agenda.

The following day, I stayed in camp to enlarge the snow cave while McGregor and Leonard pioneered the route to the lower icefall on the East Ridge. The first obstacle encountered was a knife-edge crest plummeting 300 feet away from our snowy haven before gaining elevation. They anchored rope on a more difficult section and strategically left their cache of equipment, food, and fuel at their high point.

On the fifth day, weather was questionable. After some deliberation, McGregor elected to descend to the cache he had jettisoned from his load in preparation for the rapid ascent. The cache included a handheld ground-to-air radio, our security blanket and our only hedge on the weather. Leonard and I completed the deluxe snow cave in case of retreat or a prolonged storm. Reports that night and early the next morning were promising.

We had done our homework and were equipped for climbing at 7:00 a.m. the following day. Quickly we retraced the lower portion of the route. McGregor safely led us over snow bridges and under icefalls as we followed the ridge skyward. Quickly we embraced bottomless near-vertical sugar snow. This short section was virtually a flail and unprotectable. It was a struggle, both mentally and physically. I had never experienced anything like it!

> When I wonder what I'm doing up there, cold, exhausted and terrified, I remember the words of Winston Churchill: *When you are going through hell, keep going.*
> He must have been a climber. (Marie-Odile Meunier Bouchard)

Randy's keen eyes and sharp memory solved problems before we embraced them. The ice climbing was superb, and our crampons floated on Styrofoam snow as the angle of the ridge eased off. It was the best possible of conditions for the majority of our climb, and our equipment was performing flawlessly. Remarkably the weather was holding as we approached the summit blocks in calm conditions. We had worked twelve continuous hours to cover the vertical mile. Moving together on the rope, we were more than three climbers laboring together. An undeniable link was present; a type of unspoken bonding flowed through the rope, causing the whole to be greater than the sum of its parts. What a great time to be alive, and we were sharing it with no one.

Above 13,000 feet, Leonard's upper respiratory infection took its toll. HAPE (high altitude pulmonary edema) had rendered him powerless to breathe in enough oxygen to function. Unable to muster the strength to walk the few remaining feet, Leonard rested while McGregor and I mounted the summit side by side, McGregor's first in the Alaska Range. Overcome by the icy panorama, my throat tightened; I was immensely proud of our little group. Just for that moment, I owned everything that the eye could see. I thought of my supportive family in Fairbanks that I was missing. Tears welled as I felt privileged to stand where few will stand and enjoy the brotherhood of a challenge met with and overcome by the three of us. My tears joyfully flowed for the freedom I was born into and the guidance I received from my parents, Dick and Rosalie. I was overwhelmed by the unimaginably broad expanse of the remote crystal-clear surroundings.

When we summited, I sighed in happy relief; I felt a great sense of satisfaction and excitement. And for that instant, the earth at my feet stood still. I remembered a description of the Tetons: "These are the mountains a child imagines mountains to be, of bold and grand summits, massive ice fields, of pinnacles leaping for the sky." I could see all that and more from where I stood, and it was more than I could inventory.

In my heart I was celebrating my exceptional fortune to be alive in this glimmer of time. Although our journey was only half over, I felt a great relief of tension. The mountain had been kind to me, allowing me to live through this adventure and preparation for the same. Although the sun was low, my mind recorded every image, each ray of light, the sharp cold wind on my hands and face, and my heart felt an overwhelming spiritual surge. No greater satisfaction can man experience on a moment-to-moment basis.

The leading US ice climber Yvon Chouinard reflected on climbing and mountaineering:

> In reaction, we set sail on the wide sea without motors in hopes of feeling the wind; we leave the land rover behind as we seek the desert to know the sun, searching for a remembered bright world. Paddling oar again, we turn to ride the shore break landward, walking on the waves, the smell of wild flowers meeting us on the off shore breeze. In

the process we think not what our tools can do for us but what we are capable of feeling without them, of knowing directly. We learn how far our unaided effort can take us into the improbable world. Choosing to play this game in the vertical dimensions of what is left of wild nature makes us climbers. Only from the extreme of comfort and leisure do we return willingly to adversity. Climbing is a symptom of postindustrial man.

Our extended twelve-hour journey to the summit forced us to bivouac in the open at 13,500 feet. The small summit stove hissed in the darkness as I melted snow far into the night for our nutrition and hydration. Although blowing snow on the exposed ridge froze the senses, the eyes were treated to an anomalous but glorious display. We had missed a total eclipse of the moon a few nights earlier, unaware of its 2:00 a.m. schedule. Now, in its finest grandeur, the moon glowed iridescent green! I can't believe that it was real even to this day, but in fact it was. Unable to explain this phenomenon, it captivated my attention and helped pass those long numbing hours. It was not a simple scientifically explainable green flash but, rather, a constant glow. The eerie light illuminated peaks and valley floors; it cast long spine-chilling shadows that vanished into untold wastelands of rock and ice. Partially starved of oxygen, dehydrated, weary, and malnourished, these visions are indelible in my mind.

East Ridge of Mount Hayes. Inset shows McGregor in the shade and Martin
in the sunlight at the very base of the ridge; look for the bird beak shadow.
Photo by Randy Lippincott.

Luck and weather were with us for the remainder of the trip. We carefully retraced our route to an enlarged snow cave christened Fort Levi, where we were able to radio our desire for an early departure. Aware of persistent avalanche danger due to recent snowfall, we neither lowered our guard nor breathed easily until safely back on the glacier and out of harm's way. From our perch, we noticed the landing strip had been enveloped by avalanche debris during the night. Oh well, it was a big glacier. We all felt jubilant! Like clockwork, the drone of the Cessna 185 announced the end of a near-perfect adventure. In shirtless weather, we reluctantly loaded the airplane. As we circled to gain altitude, necks craned and cameras snapped to capture the last views of our "island in the sky" and the magnificent east ridge of Mount Hayes.

Chapter Two: Spaceshot (cont'd)

Kalvan split the eighth pitch on Spaceshot to facilitate communication and just in case I needed help or encouragement. Now it was an easy climb to the end of number 9 and then fourth class scrambling to the summit ridge. It had been twelve hours since we started at the base of the climb and nine hours since we had any water.

Once both of us were secure, shoelaces loosened and the ropes coiled, we set off, traversing the steep downslopes. With minimal celebration, I looked around at the scenery and relished the feat that we had just accomplished: what a great day! We located a well-marked tree where we set up our first rappel. The descent was a series of double-rope rappels over multiple parallel cliffs. We scrambled to the climbers' right until we had to stop and set up another rappel (this is a necessary evil in a climber's view, not to be taken lightly). At the end of the day, we were tired. It was easy for us to let our guard down, and it only takes one mistake to fall to your death in the fading light. We carefully repeated the scrambles and down climbed to the following rappel for the next two hours. Soon enough we reached the road and, within minutes, were on the last bus out of the park.

We were delighted to be on our way back to the motel. Very tired and thirsty, we were the happiest guys on that full bus. Thinking about the fourteen-hour day; the wall seemed like a sweet dream, somewhat surrealistic, except for the chapped lips. That was very real. To capture the moment, we had a fellow passenger take a picture of us in our disheveled state. Anxious to put the day behind us, we were ready to shower and procure sustenance.

At the pizza place, we ordered the traditional pitcher of beer and a large pizza. We leaned back in our chairs, put our feet up, and talked about the great day that we had. My eyes are always bigger than my stomach. By the end of dinner, I was stuffed and ready for bed. You know, postprandial somnolence. One cannot make up a severe electrolyte imbalance with one large combination pizza. I was about to find out that my serum sodium and potassium levels were at all-time lows, now even more diluted by copious libation. Low potassium causes muscle irritability and can lead to uncontrollable cramping. Note to self . . .

In no time we were horizontal and the lights were out. I pride myself in being a good sleeper and fast to fall asleep. This process was shockingly interrupted by inner-thigh cramps. Controllable at first, I could almost ignore them. I *never* have had this problem, but inner thigh spasm is unheard of and, by the way, extremely excruciating. Then wave after wave of vicious muscle convulsions. Each flood of pain building on the last wave until I cried out! Kalvan thought I had been bitten by a Gila monster. At that point, all I could say was "Cramps!" I could picture the October 1981 Gary Larson cartoon with the knotted snake bolting up in bed screaming, "Charlie Horse!"

I writhed around in bed, trying different techniques to relieve the muscle spasms, biting my lip to keep from screaming out. I had knots on my knots. They were inescapable; nothing seemed to help. After about twenty minutes of my whimpering and denial, Kalvan let out a yelp. He was getting severe cramps too. Was there some sort of contagium in our room? I had to do something fast to disrupt my pain spasm cycle! I shot out of bed and started to run a hot bath while I looked for Advil and Valium in my Dopp kit. Like a lobster in a pot of boiling water, I plopped my body into the steaming bath and waited for the drugs to work. The astral projection class helped, and ultimately, I was able to fall asleep in the tub.

I awoke sometime during the night when the tub cooled or my head slipped under the water—I don't recall which. I was able to stagger back to the correct bed in my drug-induced stupor and finish the night on needles and pins. I waited for the next attack. My legs quivered, sensitive to the meat grinder they had just come through. I would have been in serious trouble without the Valium. I would have been unable to walk, and it would have been impossible for me to lie still for any given time. Truly, I was between a rock and a hard spot.

When profound sleep did come, it seemed to focus on my epiglottis and soft pallet. The prolapse of the minimally redundant flesh into my airway was subtle at first but progressive. It's as if the soft tissue had tightened during my waking hours and now was completely relaxed, swollen, and drawn into my airstream in an exaggerated fashion. The reverberations started out with a gentle throaty murmur, then at the end of the first stanza, the chorus burst forward. The decibels climbed inversely with the depth of my slumber. The chainsaw roared to life, and the sound reverberated off the walls of the tiny room. Now Kalvan could no longer ignore the harmonic convergence! He needed more than earplugs and a pillow over each ear; he needed a vacuum to place his head in. It was more than just a roller coaster—it was a freight train, a full-blown hurricane, more than a Midwestern thunderstorm. It was an F5 tornado, and there was no escaping my acoustic wrath.

The sun did rise the next day, and we were somewhat refreshed. Although the cramping did not return, I felt like it might at any moment. My inner thighs were bruised and supersensitive following the grueling night of abuse. Dehydration had taken its toll on both of us; Kalvan and I were ready to head home. The drive back to St. George felt placid compared to the day before. We never encountered a single Mustang; apparently the word had gotten out. Our return flight retraced the same route over the Grand Canyon but in much different light this time. Ever changing, awe-inspiring, the Canyon continues to captivate and amaze even the veteran explorer.

Now I felt initiated into the fraternity of big wallers. As I piloted the Cessna home from St. George, Utah, my mind wandered. I had visions of the most famous big wall in the United States—El Capitan. After my introduction on Spaceshot, I wondered, *What would it be like to "hang out" on that three-thousand-foot face for three or four days?* I really wanted to know.

The Quintessential Alaska Weekend

In 1987, I was pilot at the wheel when I crossed the Arctic Circle for the first time. The awesome view of the eastern Brooks Range that first week in June is still vivid in my mind. It turned out to be the quintessential Alaska weekend. June marks the end of winter and the beginning of summer in the Alaskan Arctic. The sun lazily circles overhead, providing desperately needed radiation to the dormant flora and fauna. There is a brief golden period after *breakup* (this Alaskan term designates the coming of spring as ice is swept downstream and melting snow turns into mud) and before the agony of mosquito season when alpine hiking is at its peak. The stable winter weather patterns give way to the more volatile thermal summer skies. Old Mr. Sol's arc rises far above his winter path with a proportionate increase in intensity. Well north of the Arctic Circle, the sun won't set again until late summer.

Glenn Elison, the Arctic Wildlife Refuge manager, suggested a unique weekend climbing trip in the eastern Brooks Range. Three of us would fly from Fairbanks to the still-frozen Peters Lake. Conveniently landing at the base of Mount Chamberlin, we could make the round-trip in three days. A third local climber was located to complete the group. Mark Wumkes had recently returned from a climbing trip to Mount Kimball and was in top form. A veteran of Alaska climbing, Mark had accumulated over 360 days climbing in the Delta Mountains of the Alaska Range.

As the pilot and co-owner of the vintage Cessna 205, I agonized over the weather for two days, while it continuously blocked our attempts to set out on our journey. We had allowed a small window for weather but had intended to use it on location. Although blue skies in Fairbanks summoned us northward, weather reports a mountain range away remained grim. At this point, Glenn canceled due to work constraints. With a halfhearted noon start and every conceivable "Alaskan toy" packed in the airplane, we took off entertaining alternate plans of soaking frustrated bodies at Circle Hot Springs.

We crossed the White Mountains at 10,500 feet as the distant silver threads of the Yukon River basin came into view. Nearly spanning the horizon from east to west, the fifth largest drainage basin in North America unfolded before us. Encouraged by the remarkable visibility, we made a beeline to Fort Yukon for a mandatory fuel stop. The small village of Fort Yukon at the junction of the Porcupine and the Yukon Rivers marked the crossing of the Arctic Circle (an imaginary line, 66° 30' north latitude, denoting the northern border of the temperate zone). Energized by continuous daylight, we pressed on to Arctic Village, typified in Bob Marshall's book *Arctic Village* as "houses almost lost in the vast, snow buried expanse of the surrounding country."

Nestled at the base of the eastern Brooks Range in the Chandelar River Basin, Arctic Village is a quiet sentinel marking the last sign of civilization between the vast interior and a coastal DEW line outpost—Barter Island on the Beaufort Sea. The isolated Arctic Village of approximately 120 people is accessible only by boat, airplane, snowmachine, or dog sled. Beyond lay the pristine wilderness of nearly eight million acres in the Arctic National Wildlife Refuge. This is the classic Alaskan wilderness at its finest, typified by rugged snow-clad mountains and broad glacial valleys.

In silky-smooth clear Arctic air at 11,500 feet, we gazed down on fluffy white clouds, lazy captives contrasted with the bold, rough peaks. Clearly able to see our route on the ground, we noted our progress on aeronautical charts. There was no GPS then and no asking directions. We relied on our maps, watch, and compass; it's what we call dead-reckoning navigation. Like virgin tourists, we were awestruck with the splendid scenery that we shared with no one. Noses pressed against the Plexiglas, we strained to memorize each new panorama as it was revealed to us. What a wonderful stimulation to the senses. The throaty drone of the old Cessna in our ears, the faint smell of oil in our nostrils, and the intense sunshine on our faces added to the mesmerizing effects of the moment. Were the insidious intoxicating effects of hypoxia taking its toll? We did, after all, feel excited and euphoric.

On the extreme right is the snowcapped Mount Chamberlin bordering Peters Lake—eastern Brooks Range, Alaska. We parked the airplane on the ice near the small peninsula at the three o'clock position of the near lake. Photo by Randy Lippincott.

Ahead of schedule because of fair weather and tailwinds, we noticed a large snowcapped peak jutting proudly above any obstructing clouds. We approached it, cautiously excited. Yes, it had to be our Shangri-la. However, our hearts sank at our first views of what appeared to be a large fogbank surrounding the base of Mount Chamberlin. Surprisingly it turned out to be our sprawling icy runway. With feelings of giddy anxiety, could this wonderful scene be ours to embrace and devour?

Excitedly we circled the scenic mountain, wildly snapping photos and making mental notes as we studied our climbing route from our bird's eye view. As we lost altitude, my anxiety climbed. We were descending to land with wheels on a patch of ice 220 miles north of the Arctic Circle during official summer. The gentleman who vouched for the quality of the solid water canceled at the last possible moment. Clear weather and warm sunshine have a relaxing effect unless you are already perspiring. As we flew low level the length of the lake, subtle irregularities in the ice loomed out at me. My mind raced to explain color changes, questionable texture, and ominous fissures in the cold white surface. Mark reassured me, "Glenn said the ice was at least four feet thick." I mentally reviewed my Titanic evacuation procedures and pulled the throttle back, allowing the trusty bird to settle onto the intrepid runway. A cold, hard surface never felt so good as I started to breathe again. We rolled to a stop in front of the G. William's Holmes Research Station and unloaded our gear, acting as though we were pulling into our own driveway after a hard day's work. I was never so relieved!

Randy Lippincott on his hands and knees kissing the "terra firma" lake ice the first week in June. Yes, it was still at least three feet thick! Photo by Mark Wumkes.

At 9,020 feet, Mount Chamberlin is the tallest peak in the Brooks Range of northern Alaska. It nourishes two pint-sized glaciers on its upper slopes. Unlike the massive mountains and rivers of glaciers in the Alaska Range, the Brooks Mountains seem to have been stunted by the intense cold of the long winters. Conversely, the perennial snow and ice suffer for only a brief period under the intense long days of summer. By the first week in June, there is little snow below the 7,000-foot level. The warm weather has melted all but the thickest ice at lower elevations. Our start from the lake to the summit would span over 6,000 vertical feet—12,000 feet round-trip. The climbing route was first ascended in 1960 and is straight forward. The weather remained clear and visibility unrestricted. The treeless plain and valleys carpeted in classic tundra appeared "well groomed," inviting us into its bosom bathed in the soft Arctic pastels of summer.

We quickly selected essential gear only. This was to be our "blitzkrieg" ascent. After a light meal, we shouldered our packs for a short march to the base of the climb. As we skirted the lake, we saw overwhelming evidence of the recent migration of the Porcupine caribou herd. Annually, part of the 180,000-strong herd passes through this glacial canyon on its way to the Arctic coastal plain and spring calving grounds. New signs of life were abundant everywhere. The remote wildlife refuge is a habitat for muskoxen, grizzly bear, wolves, caribou, moose, and Dall sheep. The tundra showed evidence of new growth, and the flora was nourished by sparkling streams and flooded with the enduring daylight. Vibrant smells laced the air announcing the urgency of the short growing season. Our faces were washed by the cool, calm, pure arctic air.

As our path grew steeper, the treeless tundra became terraced with huge boulders, punctuated with multicolored hearty lichen and an occasional bouquet of wildflowers! We stopped to eat and rest frequently, enticed by the natural tundra bed. Like house cats, we napped as the warm sun circled overhead. Refreshed and encouraged by our steady progress, we pressed on. Mark and I reached the halfway point in six hours including a one-hour nap and rest stops. At this point the ridge narrowed, and the snow was nearly continuous. Blessed with clear skies and unlimited vistas, we cached all but food, water, and parkas for the summit. Our steady climbing pace was maintained around occasional gendarmes, and we moved quickly over the firm snow. The ridge ahead of us pierced the deep blue sky as if thrust upward by the surrounding stark crags.

Water from melting snow causes steep snow slopes to lose their cohesiveness with the underlying rock. Gravity overcomes large snowfields that may spontaneously avalanche or be triggered by a man's weight. Soft-slab avalanche signs were present on most aspects of nearly every slope tempering our progress. The imminent hazards were reconfirmed on the steep upper slopes by the ominous hollow sounds we refer to as whumphs. This is a red flag for high avalanche danger. Enormous areas of snow crust settle from the climber's weight and displace vast amounts of trapped air, causing the audible sound.

Unroped for the sake of speed, we crossed high-danger areas one at a time. Experienced eyes strained for potential slide areas as the stakes increased. The ridge precipitously dropped away 1,500 feet on either side! Inching our way upward, we probed with ice axes to test the snow layers for integrity. As we reached the heavily corniced ridge, we had named cake walk, our pace quickened. Now with the peak virtually in front of us, we were halted by a gaping crevasse. Mark discovered a likely place to cross. In melodramatic fashion we leapt the gaping abyss—ice axes high overhead, straps flapping in the breeze.

Only after mandatory summit photos were taken in the calm, clear air did we realize it was 4:00 a.m. Once the view had been savored, we hollowed out a wilderness perch on the north face of the summit. Lawn chair-style we nestled in for our second one-hour nap; a meniscus of the Arctic Ocean in the distance graced our view. The silent orange disc hovered high overhead, shining down on our Cheshire cat faces. Rested and rehydrated, we started our retreat. Our descent was made in a fraction of the time. Quickly we returned to our cache at the 6,000-foot level, safely retracing our steps.

After feasting on gourmet delights (the chef's favorite was something spicy "south of the border"), we melted into prewarmed-down sleeping bags, the high morning sun energizing our human solar cells. Deprived of sleep, relaxing in our nylon cocoons, we sailed off and were quickly dreaming out of control! The remainder of the descent was expedited by traversing steep scree slopes. Virtually impossible to ascend, at the angle of repose, we literally slipped our way to the bottom glissade-style (standing up, of course).

Like two schoolboys on a field trip, we tarried: inspecting rocks, watching birds overhead, examining bleached bones, smelling the fragrant Arctic air, and feeling the tundra push back heavy feet. We easily negotiated the remaining distance along Peters Lake to the Fish and Game cabin and awaiting bunks. The Cessna patiently waited nearby, seemingly happy at our speedy return. Hot brews of cocoa and mocha were poured, and bodies were nourished. As I settled back to relax on the top bunk and play tunes on my Walkman, Mark struck out across the expansive cobbled white surface of the lake on his mountain bike. In the distance he appeared to be a radio-controlled model; his fishing pole looked like an antenna poking out of his pack.

Late that evening or early the next morning—I don't recall which—Mark returned with some pretty believable fish tales. As we wanted to avoid midday mountain storms, reluctantly we left our magic valley that morning. Clear skies allowed us to retrace our route across the Brooks Range and home unimpeded. From that day on, each June 1st I fondly recall the quintessential Alaskan weekend and yearn for a repeat performance.

CHAPTER THREE
Scenic Cruise in Black Canyon of the Gunnison
or No Country for Old Men

Yeah, OK, so we had talked of Scenic Cruise, and I was already in Colorado; was it really a good idea to do it right now? I protested that the record heat and southern exposure made it a poor choice. Couldn't we consider some other high-altitude, sun-protected, cool climb? I would dream about cold rock and how well my shoes gripped it and how good I felt climbing on it. Climbing is fun; I wanted to have fun, and I wanted to climb something that made me want to sing. Something that was not too easy, not too exposed, did not have an impossible approach, but was long enough to enjoy all day long. The predicted weather was not going to help this half-baked idea. Then just as suddenly, I was awakened by a rerun of *Groundhog Day*. Why did I have a feeling of signing up for the Bataan Death March?

It was described by the National Park Service as "Deep, steep, and narrow. Big enough to be overwhelming, still intimate enough to feel the pulse of time, Black Canyon of the Gunnison exposes you to some of the steepest cliffs, oldest rock, and craggiest spires in North America. With two million years to work, the Gunnison River, along with the forces of weathering, has sculpted this vertical wilderness of rock, water, and sky."

Legendary Colorado climbers Layton Kor and Larry Dalke began establishing big routes in the Black Canyon of the Gunnison in 1960. By 1964, they had gravitated toward one of the biggest and most intimidating walls of all: the East Face of the Chasm View Wall. Looming above one of the easiest access gullies to the Canyon on the north side, the monolithic nature of this wall must have attracted their gaze and ambitions upon their first visits to the area. They could not have guessed, as they aided and free climbed the route using the only tools available at the time, the hammer and piton, that they were creating what would eventually become one of the finest free routes in the state. A few years after the Kor/Dalke ascent, and fresh from other successes in eliminating aid from routes in the Black, Jimmy Dunn and Earl Wiggins took a sandwich, a quart of water, and a rain jacket apiece, and boldly launched a successful, 6-hour ascent. When friends asked them about their climb later, Jimmy exclaimed "We cruised it!" It has been known as *The Cruise* ever since. Lessor among Colorado climbs perhaps only to a few routes on Long's Peak in quality and challenge, *The Cruise*, and its later four-pitch variation termed *Scenic Cruise*, provide varied and difficult climbing with many memorable passages. The crux finger crack, the famous Pegmatite Traverse, and a heel-hook move onto a detached flake are only some of the treats served up by this route, the overwhelming consensus as the best in the Canyon.

Both the original *Cruise* and the *Scenic Cruise* variation are classic in nature and bear the same difficulty rating. Most modern climbers prefer the hand cracks and finger locks of the variation to the original line, which provides its crux in the form of a long and strenuous off-width crack. Dunn has by now climbed *Scenic Cruise* over 20 times, but he has never repeated the regular route that he and Wiggins first freed.[6]

I flew myself to Montrose in the Columbia 400, and Kalvan arrived commercially into Grand Junction, Colorado. We met at the Black Canyon Jet Center in Montrose to discuss our plans in air-conditioned lounge chairs. We deliberated our options and both knew of the severe heat wave that we were planning to expose ourselves to. The cavalier attitude came easily in the air-conditioned pilot lounge. After all, we hadn't come all this way to do an easy climb did we? Déjà vu—now just where had I heard that before? It was starting to feel more and more like Groundhog Day! OK, let's play What If. What would it take to climb Scenic Cruise? Kalvan felt good. I felt good. We had all the gear; let's see how it goes with an early start. Yeah, what the heck, we can do it. It was that runaway ego again. If we can dream it, we can do it.

Mount Doonerak

This was not the first time I had to make a tough decision about climbing. In 1985 on Mount Doonerak in the central Brooks Range of Alaska, it was very remote, exceptionally cold, and the consequences were extremely serious for all the members in the party. Winter mountaineering in the Arctic is a far cry from farming on the plains in Nebraska. Steve Steckmyer, Randy McGregor, and I made Mount Doonerak in the National Park, "Gates of the Arctic," the target for our winter adventure.

I had recruited an old friend, Steve Steckmyer from Seattle, Washington, along with my regular climbing partner, Randy McGregor from Fairbanks, Alaska, for the remote trip. My first Alaska climb had been Mount McKinley the previous May. Steve had done most of his climbing in the Northwest and was employed as a design engineer for Boeing in Seattle. Steve and I had attended high school together. We started skydiving at the same time and we joined the army in 1969 under the buddy plan. Later on Steve was part of an attempt to climb K2 in the Karakoram Range. Randy McGregor was a Mayo Clinic-trained anesthesiologist at Fairbanks Memorial Hospital. His prior Alaska experience had been on Mount Huntington—*The Mountain of My Fear.*

In Robert Marshall's book *Alaska Wilderness*, he relates stories of hardship and exploration of the Brooks Range. Marshall's book describes the wilderness this way:

> There is nothing to create even a flickering illusion that this is a land of milk and honey. The sheer stupendousness of the wilderness gives it a quality of intangibility which is unknown in ordinary manifestations of ocular beauty.

These inspiring accounts set the stage for this magnificent winter mountaineering saga. Mount Doonerak was a strong force that drew Marshall back to the North Fork of the Koyukuk after his first visit in 1929. Temporarily called the Matterhorn of the Koyukuk, Marshall later renamed it Mount Doonerak. Intrigued by its massive distinct silhouette, Marshall was mystically attracted to the mountain. Protected from all sides yet playfully attractive, the mountain teased him visually. Thus the Eskimo name Doonerak, which means "mischievous spirit." He had climbed most of the major peaks in the Koyukuk drainage for exploration and mapped over fifteen thousand square miles on foot. It was a nearly superhuman feat due to the boggy tundra and otherwise rugged terrain. Not until nine years later did Marshall's first and subsequent summer attempts to climb Doonerak end in failure. Isolated in the heart of the Brooks Range, nearly one hundred miles north of the Arctic Circle, she is the symbol of wilderness for all time.

Expedition planning leaves no details to chance. There is no indigenous population to rely on, no road, and no means of rescue in an emergency situation. We did not have GPS receivers or satellite telephones then. The expedition was its own best resource and its only chance for survival until the scheduled date for pickup. It was a very serious undertaking. Equipment must be adequate for temperatures encountered, and food intake must be calculated for stresses placed on the system by environmental and physical demands. Provisions for shelter must be adequate for the worst weather scenario, and pre-expedition conditioning was mandatory for a successful trip. Technological advancements make cold weather tolerable and hard climbing possible but were limited by the weight one was able to carry. Weather and snow pack are natural variables, but equipment failures must be anticipated to avoid disaster.

Although Mount Doonerak has been climbed seven times in the last fifty years, no prior winter attempt had been made. Transportation to the head waters of the North Fork in winter was by airplane, skis, snowmachine, or dog sled. The three of us and our gear were flown nonstop from Fairbanks to the confluence of Bombardment Creek and the North Fork of the Koyukuk River.

This gorge was named by Marshall for the summer rock fall along the 3,000-foot-high east face of Hanging Glacier Mountain, an imposing natural barrier.

Once deposited on the North Fork of the Koyukuk, it grew very quiet as we watched the ski-equipped Cessna 185 disappear from sight. That was nearly our last contact or hint of civilization for the next ten days. We organized gear, stepped into our skis, and moved all our supplies to the wooded mouth of Bombardment Creek. We set up camp, built an elaborate kitchen area in which we could stand to cook and melt snow. We also gathered deadwood for a primeval bonfire. Steve, Randy, and I all enjoyed this time together. Stories of previous climbs were shared around the campfire. We were quickly forming a cohesive climbing team.

The onerous ascent of Bombardment Creek was halted at the first rock band. The path of least resistance dictated that we ski around the frozen rampart. High avalanche danger ultimately prohibited circumnavigation of the precipitous waterfall. All progress was halted when the 30-degree snow slope we were traversing broke loose. We felt the entire snow slope shift and heard the incredibly ominous *whumph*, but inconceivably, it did not break free and run! It was as close to an avalanche as possible without sweeping us away. A six-inch crown wall appeared 30 feet above us, extending 100 feet ahead and behind us. It suddenly became a very tense situation. Any panic or sudden movement forward or retreat may trigger the tenuous slope, causing it to break free and carry us into the canyon far below. Any avalanche would have ended badly at this point.

The enforced halt caused the group to gingerly retreat one at a time to the river bottom. Any slip or fall at this point could mean disaster for all three of us. Randy was leading, and I was in the rear, so I had the least time exposure on the slope. Very carefully I turned around in my ski tracks and retreated to safety. Then it was Steve's turn to retreat gingerly, and then as the minutes dragged on, it was Randy's turn to do a kick step without kicking, turn around, and so very carefully retrace his tracks to safety across the seemingly endless ramp. At this point it had been sheer luck that the entire slope had not carried the three of us into the canyon far below. Later when we dug a snow pit to evaluate the avalanche conditions, we realized the depth hoar was nearly bottomless. This amounts to deep sugar snow underlying a heavy crust, the formula for a classic slab avalanche. That is, the snow beneath the surface of the hardpack outer layer has no cohesiveness to the bed rock but, rather, acts more like ball bearings.

Mountain climbing is extended periods of intense boredom, interrupted by occasional moments of sheer terror. (Anonymous)

Randy Lippincott on the first ascent of Randy's Blue Ribbon, Bombardment Creek, North Fork of the Koyukuk, Central Brooks Range, Alaska. Photo by Randy McGregor.

Elated that I was still alive and no other way around the waterfall, I took the lead up the 180-foot frozen aqua-blue obstacle. The perfect virgin ice lured me up the plastic pillar. Each blow of my ice axe was a "sinker," and each kick seemed bombproof; I loved it. This ice was perfect in every way, and the higher I climbed, the more confident I became. Somewhat foolhardily I climbed it in a single unprotected push; I used no ice screws for the onsite lead until I got to the top. At that point, I used three screws for an anchor to bring the rest of the party up the frozen cascade with heavy packs. Later the waterfall was christened "Randy's Blue Ribbon."

The third night found us laboring to erect our high camp midway between the upper and lower rock bands of Bombardment Creek; as indicated by the name, it's a death zone of rock fall in warmer weather. Light snow continued on the fourth day as the route to the south saddle of Mount Doonerak was reconnoitered. Although high camp was dug in, no high winds were encountered. Bathed in alpenglow (a salmon-pink color seen at dawn or dusk in the mountains), Mount Doonerak was in magnificent contrast to the clear evening sky. Sporting "war paint," the monolithic combatant threw down its challenge to the "Musketeers." We felt like we had solved difficult problems, moved well together, and were on schedule.

Weather deteriorated slightly on the fifth day as we awoke at 5:00 a.m. to engage the mountain. An easy route through the upper rock band was discovered, and long steep slopes were traversed to the south col. Now too close to the mountain to see the route, we mounted the Southeast Ridge. Slow but easy climbing led us to a large southwest-sloping snow field. Well-established unstable snow, like we had encountered at the start, hid high-angled loose shale rock from our vision. The amount of rotten rock increased with exposure on the extremely windblown south face. Climbing protection in the aging limestone was nonexistent, and the snow slopes were deceptively hazardous. The weathered rocks harbored no secure handholds nor ice in which to gain a purchase with an ice axe. It was hopelessly poor quality rock. Doonerak was living up to her name.

Our small party was halted less than a rope length from the summit when the snow slope that I was mounting as the lead climber started to slide. Immediately I developed tunnel vision, and my mind started to race! My only thought was that I had come a long way for it to end like this and that my misfortune could kill all three of us. I would have cut the rope, sparing the rest of the party, if I had a knife. The only thing that was possibly holding me on the mountain was my imagination! Adrenaline shot through my body; I was in a hopeless situation and did not know if my luck would hold. In a flash, I knew that although we were roped together, Steve and Randy could not possibly arrest my fall. No one was anchored to anything except the next person. I would have pulled them to their death with one false move. It would have been August before the bodies were discovered . . . .

Adhering to disintegrating rock, overlooking snow-sprayed vertical faces and verglas, we started our perilous descent. We carefully faced inward to painfully retrace our hard-earned steps and started our hazardous down climb. We agonized to avoid the mouth of the omnipresent abyss that tugged at our weary feet. On flatter ground, the relieved but disappointed climbers knew that we had made the right decision, leaving the summit for another day. Thus Doonerak held true to her name, a siren in the wilderness ready for a tricky, if not deadly, game. Later, one of the members was heard to mutter something about discretion being the better part of valor.

Somewhat deflated, we moved camp back to the North Fork and filled the remaining part of our trip with ski touring, ice climbing, and exploring. Two miles east of Bombardment Creek, a second unclaimed waterfall was discovered. Seventy-five feet of clean vertical ice beckoned to us above easy slopes. The freestanding frozen waterfall was named Nutriwik's Pick after McGregor's free solo ascent made it look routine.

Dry wood was available along the river, and old-fashioned bonfires helped cut the icy embrace of the evenings. Typical activities revolved around extended meals and hot drinks. McGregor did a fine job blending freeze-dried and "real" food into gourmet delights. Meals were celebrated with subzero Glenlivet scotch the consistency of syrup at −45° F. Poems by Robert Service were read aloud, *Thoreau's Method: A Handbook for Nature Study* was shared, and stargazing on crystal-clear nights were the favorite activities. New overflow on the North Fork would refreeze at night, causing tons of river ice to swell and snap like dry twigs underfoot. Standing on the ice, invisible fingers of sound would reverberate through the frozen surface before being audible. Frequent granddaddy cracks would echo from nearby canyon walls. Loud reports continued throughout the night to rival any modern Fourth of July celebration. Ninety-three million miles away, a coronal mass ejection was destined to be deflected by the earth's magnetosphere. Lavish dynamic northern lights danced overhead to complete the carte du jour for the senses. It was a private viewing, as if we were the last men on earth.

Wolf and Dall sheep tracks were seen. Frequent ptarmigan, Arctic hare, caribou, and moose were spotted. The raven was heard more often than seen, and the first brave flocks of migrating birds were sighted. I looked for my familiar Nebraska icon, the sandhill crane, headed for the Arctic coastal plane. Mother Nature had officially turned off the "no vacancy" sign.

Deemed a successful mountaineering trip by proof of our return, the last days were as relaxing as the first had been strenuous. In ten days we watched the Arctic Winter blossom into Arctic Spring. The warmth of the daylight was a reprieve from the cold as the sunlight increased by more than ten minutes daily. While waiting at the landing strip for the return flight, we were surprised to see our only visitors, Rob Kincheloe and friend. The duo had started an incredible journey in 1980 and were on their last three hundred miles traveling the Continental Divide from Mexico to the Arctic Ocean. It's a small world.

Bob Marshall summed up his feelings on exploration and seeking isolation:

> In the wilderness, with its entire freedom from the manifestations of human will, that perfect objectivity which is essential for pure aesthetic rapture can probably be achieved more readily than among any other forms of beauty. It is the great stimulus for mental and physical adventure alike—simply the joy of triumphing over something which is difficult to accomplish.

Chapter Three: Black Canyon of the Gunnison (cont'd)

In Montrose, we gathered our gear, packed food and water, and waited for the 3:00 a.m. alarm. We ate breakfast in the car on the long ride to the north rim of the Black Canyon of the Gunnison. There was another guided couple at the canyon rim as we started our descent at first light. The path to the bottom of the canyon was easy to find but very rocky. Some of the trail was tricky and extremely exposed. One careless step would lead to an unplanned skydiving adventure. I had failed to pack my wingsuit. Eventually we came to a fixed rope that we rappelled to the next level. More hiking and down climbing led to a second rappel, and by 7:00 a.m., we were at the base of Scenic Cruise and ready to start climbing. We made the entire approach in our climbing shoes to save weight, and I was already starting to feel the pain of the mistake. It was a deceivingly pleasant morning with a cool canyon breeze and invigorating roar of the nearby Gunnison River in the background.

The same sound that would monitor us all the way to the top of the 1,700-foot rock face—it was a complex rhythm that was both direct and an echo from the far side of the ravine. The continuous song of the river was a harsh reminder of *The Rime of the Ancient Mariner*; "Water, water everywhere, but not a drop to drink." The sound cloaked us as we climbed but just as surely drew the moisture from our bodies for its own cruel use. Yes, there was no way out but up. No shortcuts. No mulligans. No do-overs. It was all business, and it was about to get very interesting for a very, very long time.

Mount McKinley's West Buttress

Scenic Cruise was not my first major towering technical climb, but it reminded me of another big climb that I had tackled in 1984 while living in Fairbanks, Alaska. I found myself on Mount McKinley's 20,320-foot summit approximately three months after the first solo winter assent by the famous Japanese adventurer Naomi Uemura. He had been featured in National Geographic for the first-ever solo trip to the North Pole by dogsled in 1978. Although his Mount McKinley success was verified by the flag he planted on the summit, his body was never recovered. Food, his diary, and some equipment were located in snow caves at 14,200 and his 17,400-foot campsite. This area is peppered with ice caves and is referred to as the iglooplex. Japanese national climbers in search of his remains were descending as we began our climb. A grim reminder of the game we were about to play. Big mountain consequences couldn't get any more real than this. My conquest of Mt. McKinley began May 8, 1984, in Talkeetna and took fifteen days of climbing to reach the peak.

Locally referred to by its native name Denali (the Great One), it is the coldest and highest mountain in North America. It was named McKinley in 1896 for presidential nominee William McKinley of Ohio. Because of its northern latitude, it is compared to the most serious peaks in the Himalayas and is taller than Everest from its base to the summit. Because of the oblong shape of the earth's environment—flatter at the poles and taller at the equator—McKinley rises through the atmosphere at a faster rate than Everest that is considerably closer to the equator. For this reason, the Alaskan weather can be much more harsh and deadly. I remember describing the summit push as a 30-30 day. It was 30 degrees below zero, I could see 30 feet, and the wind was blowing 30 mph—a 94°F below zero windchill index. Although the West Buttress route is technically not the most difficult climb on the mountain, it claims lives regularly. The weather can place the most experienced climber in serious jeopardy very quickly.

According to Denali Park Rangers, during the first two weeks of May, the mountain was plagued by winds well over 50 mph and temperatures of 45° below zero at 17,400 feet. A total success rate of 12 percent was reported in 1984 compared with 73 percent of the climbers reaching the summit at the same time the previous year.

I climbed with five physicians, the field editor of *Powder Magazine*, and a professional guide from Fantasy Ridge Mountain Guide Service. The climb was the featured attraction of a mountain medicine symposium held by Peter Hackett, MD, in Anchorage, Alaska, that I had attended for continuing medical education credits. Six of the eight team members reached the summit on the fifteenth day of climbing, May 25, 1984. One of the climbers was escorted down the mountain from the 15,500-foot level due to acute mountain sickness. Although recovery was immediate, they were unable to make a second attempt.

From the beginning, the group was separated into three tents. Three climbers in each four-man tent, and Ray Yip and I were in a three-man tent. Ray was a pediatric hematologist from the Center for Disease Control in Atlanta, Georgia. I enjoyed Ray immensely and had a lot of fun with him. We cooked and slept in our spacious tent and worked well together. Weather was generally good for us, but we did have light snow a couple of days without wind. As we approached groups on their descent, we discovered that they had weathered their entire expedition at high camp, unable to make a summit attempt primarily due to extremely high winds and low temperatures. Over 100 mph winds on the mountain at this time of the year were common and unpredictable.

The southwest face of Mount McKinley as seen from the Kahiltna Glacier.
Photo by Randy Lippincott.

While in Fairbanks, I used cross-country skiing and hill climbing in my crampons with a heavy pack during the winter to improve my endurance at altitude. For more than two months before the climb, I dedicated myself to a seven-days-a-week cardiovascular workout schedule. This helped prepare me mentally and physically for the demanding task. My training really made the climb much more enjoyable for me. I never felt like I was about to reach my limit. However, you can't imagine how difficult climbing with a heavy pack is at 20,320 feet. It's simply breathtaking. Although conditioning is vital in preparation for this climb, some people are unable to physically acclimatize under any situation in these stressful low oxygen conditions. Deadly altitude sickness can come in the form of either pulmonary or cerebral edema. The only real treatment is to return to a lower altitude before symptoms become irreversible.

The total horizontal length of the West Buttress route is approximately 13 miles with about 13,500 feet of vertical gain. Between base camp and 11,000 feet (camp III), the route is relatively flat, and the main hazards are crevasse falls. This dictates that everyone is roped together when outside the camp perimeter. Above 11,000 feet, the route steepens to moderate slopes (35-45 degrees), the avalanche zone. The gradual approach from the Southeast Fork of the Kahiltna Glacier to the 17,400-foot level (camp VI) took us 13 days, which enhanced acclimatization. You generally can safely ascend 1,000 feet per day above 10,000 feet without suffering ill effects. Many people race up the mountain each year, and a significant percent pay the price with potentially fatal acute high-altitude sickness.

There are drugs for treatment and prevention, but descending is the only recommended cure. I personally took Diamox at the upper altitudes but still suffered a constant dull headache, agonizingly raw throat, and some mild ataxia. Physical symptoms also included tender shoulders from my heavy pack, sunburned and frostbitten nose and earlobes, and painful catching in my left knee from an old horseback-riding injury. Our mantra was "Climb high and sleep low." Since we each were assigned a 150-pound load, we would make the 1,000-foot-per-day ascent with half our gear, cache the load, and descend back to basecamp to sleep. The next day we would break camp and climb to our cache site. This method split our burden in half but doubled our distance. Therefore, we effectively climbed the mountain twice, except for the summit push from high camp.

Our only real dusting of snow fell on camp III at the base of motorcycle hill where we cached our skis and continued on crampons. While digging our tent platform, Ray discovered a snow cave—presto, an instant wine cellar. Our group had a guest "streaker" in camp while we visited with Mike Covington who had just led a client on the Cassin Ridge. Mike was owner of Fantasy Ridge Guides, the same service that we were using on the mountain. We had a very lighthearted group with balloons, masks, wintertime flashing, and our mascot was a Bob's Big Boy doll.

Above camp III we circumvented an imposing area of a huge icefall and an ominous field of séracs. Near Windy Corner, I dropped into a crevasse, but my fall was arrested by my pack. Yes, I was roped and was able to extract myself. There was no warning or evidence of what was lurking below the surface. I had no idea how big or how deep the actual crevasse was and didn't spend anytime investigating it. Check that box. At this point we were trekking at 90 degrees to the known crevasses in the area. Now it was more important than ever to know Mother Nature's rules.

We made camp at the very large 14,200-foot basin (camp IV) and at 15,000 feet (camp V) on the headwall. Although camp V is not customary today, it was used by Bradford Washburn on the first ascent of the West Buttress in 1951. The large plateau was a gathering place for climbers, and the high-altitude research facility run by Peter Hackett, MD, was also strategically located there. It was a brilliantly clear day, and Mount Hunter, at our level and directly south of our position, was majestic indeed.

The north face of Mount Hunter as seen from the 14,200-foot level
on Mount McKinley. Photo by Randy Lippincott.

We had time to explore a huge crevasse at the 14,200-foot level.
As I approached it from uphill, I had the feeling that we were on the
wrong side and halted our effort 10 feet short of the edge. After we
had circumvented the rift and repositioned ourselves on the downhill
side, I could clearly see that we had been standing on a huge 30-foot
overhanging cornice. Although it appeared sturdy enough, we saw
other sections that had broken off spontaneously and plunged the
nearly 150 feet to the bottom of the enormous ancient chasm. This
large crevasse is easily visible on the Mount McKinley National
Park brochure. The photograph was taken by Bradford Washburn
for National Geographic in 1979. I did rappel down inside the
large formation to explore and photograph it. Not exactly a benign
exercise.

The 15,000-foot headwall camp was work-intensive and sleep
depriving. Halfway up the headwall, we dug out platforms on the
45-50 degree slope to pitch our tents. This turned out to be a large
volume of hardpack snow next to a narrow crevasse in the slope.
This left little room to maneuver outside the tent, and any misstep

in either direction may have easily been fatal. Most of all, during the night, flurries of snow continuously sloughed onto the tent, causing great consternation for me. Somehow I was particularly sensitive to avalanche potential. The sound caused by the snow striking the top of the tent made an ominous noise as if to warn of a coming deadly slide. We were completely vulnerable, and I can say that this was the only truly anxious moment on the trip for me. This is where the only member of our party developed acute mountain sickness and was escorted down the mountain and back to Talkeetna.

To gain the 16,000-foot West Ridge, our group used the fixed line on the headwall for safety. We carried heavy loads, and the work was extremely tiring. It was take one step, breathe about five to eight times, then the next step and more rapid, nonstop gasping. The dry air and forced open-mouth breathing made the back of my mouth raw and is referred to as altitude throat. The vista after reaching the ridge was worth it. Both the magnificent Mount Foraker to the west and Mount Hunter to the south were wonderfully contrasted with the surrounding mountains and endless vistas.

The official death zone is 24,000 feet; that is, there is not enough available oxygen to sustain human life for any period of time. My personal experience is that there is no civilization above 17,000 feet and that I lost all appetite at camp VI. I had to force myself to eat. There was no question in my mind that I was suffering from altitude-induced anorexia. With low levels of oxygen, it is difficult for your body to metabolize fat and protein. Once anorexia has set in, your body turns into a catabolic state; you start feeding off your own fat and muscle mass. We were rationed five thousand calories per day up to this point. Now I found it an effort to consume one thousand calories per day at 17,400 feet, a major shift. These calories are both necessary for the strenuous work performed and "fuel for the furnace," to keep the body warm. Now in a muscle wasting situation, high camp becomes my own personal death zone with the clock ticking.

After one weather day at the 17,400-foot level, camp VI (due primarily to visibility) I was anxious to make my summit bid. Ray had run out of desire at that point. I believed that he was low on energy due to the altitude-induced anorexia. The party was split in two. The first half was ready to leave for the summit immediately, and the second half would go if and when they could get their act together. I explained to Ray that he could do it if I loaned him my secret weapon. I had a thermos. All he had to do was make soup for his journey, and he would be energized and hydrated enough to make the summit. I made him promise to give it his best effort if I were to leave my summit leverage with him. As it turned out, my water froze solid in my pack. I found myself very tired and dehydrated on the summit. Ray, on the other hand, was in fine shape and completed his summit push uneventfully.

After departing camp VI, it was an easy trek to Denali Pass carrying light packs. The summit push was longer than I had expected, (2½ miles one-way), but our group maintained its pace. The five-hundred-calorie breakfast and lack of fluid intake for the day in the most extreme and dry environment took its toll on me. I suffered great disappointment after reaching the second false summit on the ridge to the true south summit. My feelings were unspoken, as I was traveling alone in my mind, isolated by the harsh cold wind and extreme effort to communicate with anyone ahead or behind me. If there had been a third false summit, I am not sure if I could have gone on much further.

Our 20,320-foot celebration was short-lived but sweet. Everyone simply had to keep moving. We took time for the obligatory photos and immediately started back. We had a euphoric reunion at camp VI when everyone returned safely and triumphantly.

From left to right: Randy Lippincott, PA-C; Bob Slozen, guide; Dave Graham, MD. 20,320 feet, summit of Mount McKinley, May 25, 1984. Photographer unknown.

The journey off the mountain was easy with quiet elation and gravity. It only took us two days to return to the Southeast Fork of the Kahiltna and wait for our late-night ride with Lowell Thomas Jr. I recall vividly the vibrant green color of the forest and nearly overwhelming aroma of the vegetation during our low-level flight back to Talkeetna. My senses had been shut down for over two weeks. I had been exposed to no smells and blinded by the overwhelming color of white in the sterile environment. Following the short flight back to Talkeetna, I arrived in Fairbanks at 5:00 a.m. in broad daylight. The climb was as much as I'd hoped for and more than I expected.

The things that plagued me for the following two weeks were that I was too hot to sleep under the covers, my metabolism had been so revved up, and I felt like I had the energy to run a marathon. My body was supercharged; the red blood cells had been stimulated by the high altitude (natural doping) to carry more oxygen, so I had lots of reserve energy. All of that changed at the end of several weeks, and I didn't schedule any grueling events for myself. I had been to the mountain and returned.

West Ridge of Mount Hunter as seen from the airstrip on the
Southeast Fork of the Kahiltna glacier. Photo by Randy Lippincott.

Chapter Three: Black Canyon of the Gunnison (cont'd)

At this point, the beginning of Scenic Cruise was easy to find, almost as easy to identify as the poison ivy under our feet. The top of the first pitch already found us in the sun. Comforting at first, the southern exposure would test our grit by day's end. Although moderate in difficulty, the pitches were long and mostly continuous with rare easy moves. Soon we were sweating in the still air.

All morning we moved with intention. Climb, belay, climb, belay; we moved rhythmically as a single unit in silence. Route finding was not always straightforward, but we progressed upwardly until pitch number 5. At that point, it was a dicey traverse with some interesting, if not difficult, face moves. The sun baked the rock. My shoes were not as effective in the heat as when we first started, so I had to work my upper body harder, sweat more, expend more electrolytes, and push the envelope. Chalk to dry sweat from my hands was important for a good purchase on the rocky holds.

By one o'clock, we were starting the seventh pitch out of thirteen; time started to blur. The overhanging corner with a 5.10+ exit was made exponentially more difficult when Kalvan was overcome with cramps. First, finger locking in his right hand, where he had to physically force the fingers straight with his left hand. Next the calves joined the protest, striking at the least opportune time. Urgently he would slam in a piece of pro, yell "take," and hang on the rope until the spasm had passed or the muscle could be stretched out! Kalvan pleaded for relief as he baked in the stagnant air. He complained bitterly of the excruciating salt crystals that formed in the corner of his eyes and nose. Crippling dehydration advanced as rivulets of perspiration trickled from under my helmet.

We were well past the point of no return; you see we started the day with a 1,700-foot descent to the bottom of the remote canyon (this would make it a total of 3,400 vertical feet for the 17-hour day, overall that is 200 feet per hour). There was nowhere to go but up and nowhere to hide from the sun! At noon we used the last of our water. Next it was my turn as irritable muscles twitched, but not to the point that Kalvan had suffered. Under my breath, I mentioned something about it being a dry heat. I watched the sun painfully inch across the sky with shifting shadows, like the condemned, fixated on the hour hand. I felt that my ninja smoke had just run out. As it turned out, the climb was replete with unexpected obstructions.

A small breather came as the climbing eased somewhat on the eighth and ninth pitches. My brain started to wander. I was losing enthusiasm. Now, without water, any sort of nutrition was nearly impossible. I could chew it, but I didn't have enough saliva to swallow it. The body slowed, and the thinking process was impeded. My enthusiasm waned; my brain swelled. All I could think about was closing my eyes and taking a nap in the shade—anything to escape the relentless, exhausting high temperature. It was a virtual convection oven. My clothing gave me no protection from the penetrating heat. I felt as though I had reached Malebolge, the eighth circle of hell in Dante's *Inferno,* and was struggling to escape its blast-furnace embrace. I had to believe that it was possible for me to move in one direction only, and that was up.

Randy Lippincott on Scenic Cruise, our first real break, about 6:00 p.m., after climbing eleven hours. Photo by Kalvan Swanky.

We took our first real break on a comfortable ledge at the beginning of pitch 10. It was nearly 6:00 p.m., and after eleven hours of climbing, I was more than willing to bivouac right there! We had been out of water for six hours. I was parched and reasoned that we should spend the night on the ledge, rest up, and the world would be "right as rain" in the morning. I just wanted a breather. Tired after the day of deprivation, I was thinking of an "easy" classic climb. I wanted to go on an outing that was fun, not intimidating, had great quality rock, and was as aesthetic as they come in the contiguous United States.

The Big Steep

Such a climb for me was the Grand Teton, sometimes referred to as the Big Steep. It was 4:33 a.m., August 2001, as the tires lifted off the Deer Valley runway for Page, Arizona, on our way to Jackson Hole, Wyoming. A light tailwind, silky smooth air, and a cool flow from the vents made for a great start. At altitude, I trimmed the airplane—the stereo was cranking out "Graceland" by Paul Simon—and I handed the controls to my copilot. I dimmed the cabin lights and settled into my seat with a sense that it wouldn't be long before we would see the first hint of orange over the horizon.

I looked into local bouldering and rock climbing in January 2001 when I wanted to revisit my old discipline. It began with a couple of Sierra Club outings. Soon I met Jim Sowden, and we started climbing together regularly. As confidence grew, we decided to try an alpine ascent of one of the *Fifty Classic Climbs of North America*. Routinely we would boulder during the week and climb native rock on the weekends. It had been a long, hot summer for us, and we welcomed the cool temperatures that Wyoming offered.

The assent of the 13,770-foot Grand Teton was a fabulous outing. My climbing partner, Jim Sowden, and I made the six-hour flight to Jackson Hole in two parts. First we flew four hours to Salt Lake City, where we stayed and climbed in Little Cottonwood Canyon—my old stomping ground. Unfortunately Jim sprained his ankle while bouldering on our very first warm-up climb, which hampered our practice activities. We did enjoy a spending spree at REI and the Black Diamond store in Salt Lake City. I purchased new rock shoes, a Marmot rain/climbing/ski jacket for half price, and some climbing books.

While in Salt Lake we slept at 9,500 feet. At the very top of Little Cottonwood Canyon, above the Alta Ski Resort, we lounged for two days to help us acclimatize. It was a nice cool shakedown and lent itself to some short, scenic hikes. I was unable to contact any old friends, but we had a great time sightseeing and breathing the mountain air.

The flight in my Cessna to Jackson Hole Wyoming was one hour and fifty minutes. We photographed and checked out the nearly 14,000-foot peak from the 11,000-foot level prior to landing. What a beautiful country we live in. The peaks are breathtaking and more awesome each time I visit them. We picked up a rental car and headed to the Star Valley Ranch where Sharon and Jim Chumley, my high school wrestling coach, were kind enough to let us bunk while they were in Alaska on a cruise. We read and lounged, which gave Jim's ankle a few more days to recover for the big event. On the satellite, we picked up *Mutiny on the Bounty* and *True Grit* for the evening entertainment.

> As a kid, I knew two things to be self-evident. Flying: Believe it and it'll happen. Superpowers: Bound to be something—spinach or whatever will do the trick. Climbing is my flying and coffee is my spinach. (Peter Croft)

On Wednesday, we registered at the Ranger Station for a camp spot on the lower saddle of the Grand Teton that day. It was a six-hour approach for us with all our climbing and camping gear. With the parking lot at 6,000 feet, the saddle at 11,300 feet, and an 8-mile approach, we were ready for an early dinner and bed by the end of a day of strenuous boulder hoping. The trail was not that developed. On Thursday, August 2, 2001, we woke to howling winds, and I was not anxious to venture onto the south face of the Grand Teton to be blown off! We had a late breakfast and, after putting it off as long as possible, made a decision to go for it.

Outside the tent, we surveyed our gear and the route in the gusty conditions. Our minimum items included rock shoes, a harness with locking carabiner and belay device, a chalk bag, 50 meters X 10.5 mm rope, rain gear, warm hats, gloves, a headlamp, a single pack, and four liters of water. The technical gear rack included a selection of small to medium Camalots (mechanical camming devices to anchor the rope), six slings, six quickdraws, medium stoppers, size 8-10 hexentrics, extra carabiners, two daisy chains, and a nut pick for extracting stuck "pro." This is a small hook used to remove stubborn nuts or stoppers out of cracks too small for one's finger to extract.

The idea of clean climbing is to ascend unencumbered by pitons and the hammer. Repeated use of these stout metal pins over the years in cracks eventually changes the nature of the climb for those who follow. Current practices dictate that the climber removes or cleans his gear (protection) from the rock as the second is belayed up by the leader. This can be done safely in areas where cracks or bolts are sufficient. Clean climbing virtually leaves no trace of the climber on the mountain. Nothing that I have pursued gives me quite as good a feeling as rock climbing, and I don't mind repeating this wonderful quote here:

> Mountains are fantastic examples of the power and mystery
> of nature, and the routes we climb on them are expressions
> of all that is best in the human spirit. (Michael Kennedy)

Our primary objective was the Exum Direct but considered the Petzolt Ridge after talking to park rangers. It was because of logistics and the late start we decided for the more expeditious traditional Exum Route via Wall Street. I think it was the right decision, as we started the approach a little before 9:00 a.m. and the technical climb on the Exum Ridge around ten o'clock. We donned our climbing shoes and harnesses, and roped up on Wall Street. I started out with the hand traverse at the exposed gap, pausing long enough to gaze down between my legs into the abyss. Yes, it was breathtaking. Jim led off with the Golden Stair, and our route finding was OK until we bypassed the friction pitch (the crux) on the upper section.

Technical sections were short, and overall, Jim did a good job of "pro" placement. However, at one spot on a particularly dicey point of exposure, he popped his first piece without knowing it. Because he had not set the nut in the crack, as he moved above the protection, the rope pulled the stopper out of the fissure and it slid all the way down the rope to me. I did not disturb Jim's progress with any useless esoterica. Had he known what had happened, it may have broken his concentration and momentum. Safety may have been more compromised by the verbal distraction. "Welcome to the deep end of the pool."

Near the last technical pitch close to the summit, something caught my eye. As I extended my neck, I focused on a beautifully sleek white glider. The pilot was using air currents off the face of the Grand Teton for lift. Somewhat of a technologic dichotomy—he was close to 14,000 feet and sailed right over my head without effort or sound. It made me realize that tools aided our progress on the rock as his journey through the air was made possible by a nonmotorized machine. His hands on synthetic controls as my fingers caressed the natural rock. His tennis shoes applied pressure to the full-sized metal rudder pedals as my tightly bound feet danced on tiny stone footholds.

Overall our teamwork, communication, and ropework was well coordinated. Our equipment was adequate, the rock was in excellent shape, and we both tolerated the altitude without any ill effects. Thankfully Jim's ankle wasn't problematic. We both were able to wear our rock shoes for the duration, which made moving on the ridge safe and easy. The exposure was fun and exciting with an occasional 1,500-foot sheer drop off. Partway up the Wind Tunnel and most of the upper ridge, we safely moved together, unroped.

We arrived at the upper snowfields and the summit at 2:00 p.m. Our visibility was unrestricted, and we could even see the fires in Yellowstone—nearly one hundred miles away. The volcanic-looking smoke was being pumped upward to 20,000 feet—well above our vantage point. This was Jim's first alpine summit and his first multipitch climb. We took pictures, visited with some other climbers on the summit, and marveled at the awesome panorama. I remembered other summits I had visited in all sorts of weather. This had to rank as one of my best views.

"I felt part of some great movement, one of infinite scale, too grand to see but only to feel in the night's wind" (Mugs Stump, North Buttress of Mount Hunter, 1981).

The descent had a thrilling 120-foot free rappel, and it was nearly 5:00 p.m. when we reached our little blue tent. It wasn't long before we were horizontal and started the rehydration process with cocoa, a main course of black beans and rice, and then some nice blueberry cobbler!

Even climbers are subject to basic needs. We were privy to the privy at 11,300 feet, a two-holer for those old enough not to need an explanation. The out-of-doors facility sat on the west side of a sizable boulder open to the earth and heavens. Apparently it was designed as open air to facilitate servicing with a helicopter. As I sat on the throne, my view to the west was spectacular and unimpaired. What more could a climber ask for? I literally watched the sun go down from that inviting seat. As long as one was not concerned about his own exposure, the vista tended to protract the event.

The next day, we slept in, and the trip back to the car was a long four-hour traumatic downhill hike. It was as hard on the knees as the heavy pack was on the already-sore shoulders. We were approached by a couple on the trail who asked us for a ride to the highway, which we were obligated to accommodate. By the time we looked for them in the parking lot, they were nowhere to be found. Later at The Pizza and Pasta in Moose Junction, we learned they had caught a ride with a five-time astronaut. Damn, stood up for an astronaut; I wished I had a nickel for every time I heard that story.

We checked in at the American Alpine Club Climbers Ranch for six dollars a night and headed out for pasta and cold beer. From our seat in the restaurant, we watched thunderclouds roll in and lightening pick away at the majestic peak. Our timing had been impeccable. Like my flight instructor used to say, "It's better to be down here wishing you were up there than up there wishing you were down here." He was right! After lunch we showered at the Ranch, took a nap, and then headed into Jackson Hole that night for a sit-down dinner, some pool table recreation, and general people-watching. What a friendly village.

Unfortunately, the trek took its toll on our poorly conditioned legs, and we didn't feel the need for any additional climbs or even the effort of local fly-fishing, which we were prepared to do. Jim also wanted an extra day to unwind before returning to work, so we reluctantly packed and headed for the airport. After waiting our turn between jets, we departed the airport and headed south up the wild and scenic Greys River. Our route went over the sleepy village of Heber, Utah, along the eastern border of the Wasatch, and through Provo Canyon. We stopped in Richfield, Utah, for fuel to insure against any unplanned off-airport landing.

As we reached the Grand Canyon, we had to deviate around scattered thundershowers. The eastern portion of the canyon was smoke-filled. As we approached, we noticed the fire generating the white cloud was south of the canyon and the wind was from the south. Apparently, heavier air was pushing the smoke into the canyon. From our vantage point, the smoke looked like Niagara Falls pouring into the insatiable abyss. A setup for a classic Ed Mell—the afternoon light, smoke, and prominent thunderstorm was a striking sight to behold. Our six-and-a-half hour flight home was straightforward until crossing into Arizona. We were forced to divert seventy miles west of Prescott just to avoid thunderstorms north of Phoenix. In Scottsdale, we were greeted with gusting wind and blowing dirt—the classic haboob.

> Limitations live only in our minds. But if we use our imaginations, our possibilities become limitless. (Jamie Paolinetti)

Chapter Three: Black Canyon of the Gunnison (cont'd)

Kalvan was confident that if we maintained our pace on Scenic Cruise, the difficulty was only moderate, and we could safely complete the route sometime that night. We knew exactly where we were on the 1,700-foot face. Now we readied our headlamps and set out in the fading light. The next five pitches were each distinctive enough that route finding was not a problem in the dark, and Kalvan could easily reach into his limitless repertoire of rope tricks. We did manage to maintain a modicum of safety; however, I had a close call with some cactus near the top of the climb in the inky struggle.

Every other minute, I would think about the chest of ice water and Gatorade in the trunk of the car. That is what kept me going. I would obsess how it would feel on my lips and tongue. How refreshing it would be to gulp the life-giving fluid. I could drink as much as I wanted! OK, now back to reality. Was that Kalvan yelling, "Off belay"? Was it my turn to address the now-cooling rock with furtive movements and tender fingers? My calves were sensitive after overstretching them ten thousand times in succession and feet that had been in the meat grinder for seventeen hours. Yes, I climbed with the focus of the headlamp. It helped define my world to the exclusion of anything else but, at the same time, limited my awareness and options to upward progress. I recalled something a mountaineer in Alaska had once told me, "It don't gotta be fun to be fun" (Carl Tobin). It was only natural that Steppenwolf's "Born to Be Wild" endlessly looped through my head.

The final pitch was straight up and over the spectators' guardrail at the Chasm View Nature Trail. How freaky would that be during the day if there were tourists present? I could just hear a little boy turn to his father asking, "Are those guys coming into the country illegally?" It was not your typical last moves to a big climb, but it was reassuring that, in fact, we made it! Now with all adrenaline spent and dry as a bone, we both shut down. After pulling the last of the rope up, we fell flat on our backs in the dirt, looking straight up into the heavens; thankful to have completed the test, we felt bucolic. Hubris was simply not in our vocabulary. I had not one scintilla of energy left in me; I was spent. Now my focus shifted to agonizing feet and the five-eighth-mile trek back to the car on the gravel road. I loosened my climbing shoelaces as much as possible and started my march in a most ginger fashion. Kalvan took his shoes off and, in a very stoic manner, walked barefoot on the gravel road back to the car.

It was most embarrassing as we consumed the ice-cold drinks with abandon. It took extra time for me to painfully tie my tennis shoes with bruised and swollen fingers; I might as well have been using my elbows. The wonderfully huge night sky distracted and enveloped us. It seemed friendly and reassuring to me as I stood firmly on the ground gazing at the heavens. Next my mind shifted to the horizontal mode; sleep would be well deserved tonight, but first it was a visit to the outhouse and a happy interlude. As I pondered my position on the bench, I didn't think that the "third day of the condor" would qualify as a hat trick.

Avalanche

My bones were tested by Mother Nature when I triggered an avalanche in 1986 while skiing in the backcountry; it made me anything but happy. I had seven years of big mountaineering experience under my belt at the time. Within the prior two years, I had attended an Avalanche Awareness and Backcountry Avalanche Hazard Evaluation Rescue Technique workshop. I also had personally been involved in two prior avalanches. These were spontaneous, not triggered by myself. Both earlier incidents were experienced on vertical ice. I remember that Terry (Lobo) Loboschefsky and I were just above the apron on Stairway to Heaven in Provo Canyon, Utah. I was leading on the second pitch when Lobo yelled "Avalanche!" We were always pulling jokes on each other, and whoever heard of an avalanche on vertical ice, but somehow I knew he was serious this time. I looked up and saw the slope in free fall 1,000 feet above me. Thankfully Lobo was well off to the side as he belayed me out of harm's way.

I focused; quickly I kicked each crampon into the ice for a good purchase and then did the same first with my right axe and then my left. Instinctively I placed my helmet between the two axes, pressed my body into the cold, hard surface, and prepared for the worst. The heavy snow pummeled me, but fortunately, no trees or rocks were in the white surprise. After being soundly thumped by the mass of speeding snow, the bulk of it was over in about twenty seconds. The avalanche came in a crescendo of waves as my mind raced to anticipate the danger yet to come. However, I was able to cling to the vertical surface; like gum to the bottom of a chair, I wasn't going "gently into the good night." There was simply no time for fear. All the while, Lobo was documenting the onslaught with a sequence of black-and-white photos. I had not placed an ice screw yet, so I guess the belay was somewhat of a moot point if I were swept off the ice. The counterpoint is that the rope would have made it easy to locate the body. I was able to down climb to Lobo, and we safely hiked back to the car because I was ready for a drink.

Series of avalanche photos on Stairway to Heaven, Provo Canyon, Utah circa 1976. Randy Lippincott leading, about 35 feet up without any pro placement. Fortunately Lobo was belaying off to the side, out of harm's way. If I had been swept off, it would have been a 70-foot whipper! Photos by Terry Loboschefsky.

On February 8, 1986, at approximately 1:45 p.m., I was traveling with the Alaskan Alpine Club on the terminal moraine of the Canwell Glacier south of Delta Junction, Alaska. We had experienced extremely warm winter weather in Fairbanks. I knew that the Delta and Black Rapids Regions were also experiencing similar weather. No signs of obvious recent avalanche activity were noted in the area. The weather over the preceding twelve hours had been snowy and extremely windy adding to the regional wind transport. On the approach to the glacier, frequent hollow sounds referred to as "whumphs" were experienced on flat terrain—a major red flag for high avalanche danger. The temperature was thirty-four degrees Fahrenheit when I left the car on my skis, another red flag. The weather was overcast, windy, and it had been somewhat warmer during the night—all very ominous signs.

I agreed to break trail for the local group, which I had not previously planned to join. The objective of the outing was for the Fairbanks students to build overnight snow caves. Separated from the group on a southern aspect of the extreme northern portion of the glacier (now the lateral moraine), I tried to find a vantage point to evaluate the area. The main body of the group was traveling on a ridge approximately 150 yards distant, parallel to, and 35 yards higher elevation than me.

Since I was lighter equipped and moving much faster easterly along a 45-degree slope above a crevassed region, I noticed the snow composition change and simultaneously slough under my skis. At the same moment, I felt the entire slope give way. I looked up and noticed a 15-inch crown wall nearly 150 feet above my starting position had developed, and the entire slope was accelerating downhill. My reflexes caused me to attempt a downhill turn to ski out of the avalanche. Somewhat apprehensive, knowing that crevasses were below me, my skis were already buried under heavy snow that acted like an anchor. The effort resulted in a downhill face-plant in the white churning mass. My right ski remained oriented; however, my left ski wind milled clockwise through 200 degrees. This caused great torsion on my left tibia, and I was expecting a painful snap when it fractured. I was instantly engulfed up to my head as I traveled down the slope. Now I was only an observer along for the ride.

From the very start of the slope movement till cessation of all motion, my mind was on a linear trajectory to reality. My only thought in my progressive state of helplessness was "So this is how it's going to end." I was resolved to my situation; I knew it was my own fault and admitted it. Powerless and overcome by the objective momentum of the universe, I was destined to be the first to the scene of the accident.

My mind had given the order to turn downhill to ski out of danger, but when suddenly engulfed, I already believed that in the stillness and developing darkness, the final chapter would quickly come to an end in quiet desperation. I had already accepted my fate, but when all motion stopped, my left hand was up to my face, and I could see light. With a little effort, I flicked snow away with my hand so I could breathe. My only thought was a possible second wave of snow, and any hope of survival or self-extraction would be snatched from my grasp in an asphyxiating surge of white death. It would be suffocation through double jeopardy and just pure bad luck. But, again, someone was watching over me.

Through members of the Alaskan Alpine Club who had not witnessed the avalanche, I was able to gain assistance. They only noticed me after hearing my cries for help. It was an unnatural act for me and felt awkward or just plain wrong for me to cry for help. Later I discovered that the initial person that heard me shout had poor vision and was unable to locate my exact position. Luckily he found another student with normal vision. At first they thought I had stepped into a hole. My best estimate of avalanche time was 10-15 seconds; my calculation for help to arrive from only 150 yards away was approximately 8 minutes. My initial call for help was undetected primarily because of gusting wind conditions. I believe the possibility of self-extraction during the remaining daylight hours were slim; twenty-four hours was more realistic.

After extrication, observation of the bed surface revealed a convex slope with the uppermost 20 feet near the crown wall being the steepest and under the most tension. Surrounding scrub oak vegetation was deceptive as the wind pillow that I triggered was void of vegetation. I was not carrying my beacon since I had planned to travel alone. It was a very solemn and introspective drive home for me. Paradoxically I remember the vivid contrast between a very lively show of the wonderfully colorful aurora borealis that night and the gloom of my near-death experience. It was the stark juxtaposition between the visually pleasing light displays that represented the lethal energy from the sun that was actively being deflected by the earth's magnetic field. As a tempest raged within me, I was witness to a silent solar storm erupting overhead. Again I was painfully aware of my manifest insignificance in nature.

When I returned home, I discovered that my family was away. At that point, I took a long hot shower, ate some chicken noodle soup, and watched *The Man Who Shot Liberty Valance* in silent reflection.

"What is behind you is forgotten. You can't remember danger and difficulty when it is behind you" (Wanda Rutkiewcz).

Again, I was happy to be alive.

Chapter Three: Black Canyon of the Gunnison (cont'd)

From the north rim of the Black Canyon of the Gunnison, Kalvan and I crawled into the rental car and headed to the motel in Montrose. However, before reaching Crawford, he unexpectedly yelped, shot back in his seat, and tried to straighten his right leg! Overtaken by severe cramping, he was unable to control the gas pedal with his foot. As Kalvan abruptly pulled off the road, he turned to me and said, "Randy, can you drive us home? I just can't do it." Yes, as it turned out, that part of my body was still working. We didn't feel like eating anything, so we headed directly to the motel. After requisite electrolytes, a hot shower, and all the drugs we could muster, I lay down at midnight. Sleep did come, but I was anxious that I might be visited by Gary Larson's "snake monster"—oh please no . . .

The next morning found us happily consuming calories at IHOP. Kalvan and I said our good-byes at the airport, and I flew myself back to Eagle, Colorado. My wife, Joyce, picked me up at the airport and announced that she had planned a hike with her sister Sue and brother-in-law Richard Jones. As it turned out, I was the butt of all jokes of kinesiology. My painfully stiffened gait that morning looked like something out of a Frankenstein movie. After seventy-two hours, I had worked most or all the lactic acid out of my muscles and almost felt normal except for some torn and sensitive skin on my fingers. I guess that's why they call it Yosemite for grown-ups.

Now that I am safely back home—rested, cleaned up, living in air-conditioned comfort—I can reflect on my recent past. It has been a passage that has taken me from the farm in Nebraska to the summit of McKinley in Alaska. It has been an interesting journey. Filled with self-induced hardships but equally blessed with a lifetime of good friends, interesting work, and privileged opportunities. I believe that my father taught me the Midwestern work ethic by example. I was never given anything but, rather, worked hard for all my good fortune in life. As I look at the man in the mirror, sometimes I see the adventurer, sometimes I see the technician, sometimes even the Dos Equis man. Whether I've been the farmer, the soldier, an iron worker, the aviator, a Physician Assistant in orthopedics, the climber, the hunter, the adventurer, or the author, life is good, and it's been a fabulous ride.

LEVITATION 29

It was to be our practice climb for El Capitan. You know—big wall, multipitch confidence builder. Kalvan Swanky, Mike Shea, and I drove to Las Vegas. Everyone knows "what happens in Vegas stays in Vegas"—well, this mostly took place outside of Vegas in Red Rocks, so I feel as if I am not breaking "the code." We checked into the Red Rocks Casino in time for a steak dinner and a reserve bottle of red wine. It is "only the best for the boys when on the road." Anxious for the climb, we retired early and were up promptly the next morning. Red Rocks recreation area opened at 6:00 a.m., and we were there waiting under a cool, crisp sky, Starbucks in hand. We drove around the loop to Oak Creek Canyon and parked the car for the arduous hike in.

We had gear, water, and food for the big day. The map description told us it was an average three-hour approach with no real trail. Indeed, the river drainage was rugged. At first it was just boulder hopping with the moderately heavy pack. Then the canyon steepened, and the boulders grew to truck-sized. To go around the boulders was to bushwhack in dense brush and thickets of the Rubicon approach. This got old very quickly. Kalvan and Mike maintained the pace as I slowed somewhat. Ultimately we found our way to the steep slabs below Eagle Wall leading to the base of the climb. At this point, I was only 100 yards behind the pair but closing the gap quickly.

This was a huge canyon with majestically towering walls. The vista across the valley was spectacular with multicolored rock begging to be explored. The higher we climbed on the approach, the bigger and more austere the vista. At this point, Kalvan had already reached the base of the climb, Mike was within 20 yards, and I was 10 yards behind him. The steep ramp transitioned to broken terrain via an exposed dicey ledge. Not as tired as I was concerned with my footing, I paid little attention to my hands that I thought I was using only for balance.

The last move that I remember on the narrow ledge was guarded by a large suitcase-sized boulder. Unwittingly I applied just enough pressure on it with my left hand as I passed to pull it free. Apparently it was only teetering in position, waiting for my passing touch. I remember being ejected from my stance as my forward movement was radically altered by 90 degrees! My position midair was a backward dive with some left-upper-torso rotation built in. That is where the 250-pound rock was applying force. I recall pushing off or, at least, separating from the rock after the first bounce. I sustained a crushing blow to my left chest and my left hand, in particular my PIP (middle joint) of my long finger. Freed from the stony intruder, I was airborne again. I did a second backflip midair and landed face up, head down, a considerable distance downslope. Instinctively I had the sense to lie motionless. Before the pain could set in or the blood really began to run, I turned my head to the right, and there was the obstacle of my fear—a giant jumping cholla cactus. If I had landed one foot to my right, I would still be picking cactus spines out of my body to this day.

I let the event sink in, evaluated my situation for continued danger, and then mentally surveyed my injuries. This levitation thing simply was not working out for me. Controlling the bleeding was not an issue. I had a bandanna that I placed on my hand as a dressing that also helped immobilize my fingers. I didn't really know if I had a fracture, but if I did, it was compound. That would be a poor diagnosis for my hand because it would require surgery to irrigate out the wound and possibly screw the fragments together. My back had been protected from the very rocky slope by my form-fitting pack and the fact that I had a three-liter bladder of water in it. This helped convert my momentum into a kind of downhill springboard. Fortunately I was also wearing my helmet, so I avoided a pesky head injury. Because I was twisting midair, my chest injury was a glancing blow, but the left hand was a crush injury between the boulder and something on the ground; it was starting to throb.

Mike had witnessed the entire event—the tandem flight with the boulder, the Cirque du Soleil backflip, and then the motionless body. At first he was wishing for a camera to put it on YouTube but then realized that it had been a serious event, and hey, he didn't have connectivity anyway. I was able to slowly get up and climb to his position to inventory my physical injuries. I was surprised that the abrasive rock had inflicted bloody lacerations wherever it had made contact. I was going to need plenty of hydrogen peroxide to get all the gore off my clothing.

The entire event had occurred out of Kalvan's view. By the time we made it up to him, he was ready to start the ascent. After a cursory survey, he agreed that climbing for me was out of the question. Although I was still feeling a bit of shock, I tried to put on the macho face. I did beg out of the climb as I reasoned that it would be impossible for me to make the ascent one-handed.

I watched Mike and Kalvan climb the first five-or-so pitches and then reasoned that it would take me longer to hike back to the car in my battered condition. The return route was unhurried, but my hand was throbbing, and I was thinking about the ice in the trunk of the car that I needed to soak my hand in. The route down was easier as I remembered the tricky parts of the trail, and some of it was actually fun. At the car, I started with a timed ice plunge for my hand and augmented it with alcohol and drugs.

The car ride back to town was supplemented pharmacologically which acted synergistically with the alcohol and my current narcotic blood levels. If I felt pain and my hand and chest throbbed, I didn't care. To hear the story from Mike and Kalvan, their journey was much more amusing than mine. Everything improves with a shower, and soon we were sitting down for dinner. I did have the good sense to excuse myself and return to the room for more ice and to elevate my hand. Kalvan's boys' night out lasted into the wee hours of the morning. I'm not sure if he got his $1,500 worth of recreation, but that morning, again I was the only one that was in a condition to drive home—even in my traumatized and bloodied state!

"Most sports require only one ball."

—seen on a T-shirt with a picture of a climber

EPILOGUE or
The Rocky and Bullwinkle Show

In true Paul Harvey spirit, here is "the rest of the story." These climbing stories have not been my only or worst encounters with dehydration troubles. Abandoned in the Alaska wilderness after shooting, skinning, and guarding a full-sized bull moose, I nearly became a casualty as a result of profound stress dehydration and sepsis. The owly condor was preceded by the mangy moose in my lethal menagerie.

It was the fall of 1985, and it was moose season in Fairbanks, Alaska. My hunt had been successful the year before but not as smooth as I had planned. This was not going to be any different; Alaska has a way of throwing you a curveball when you are not looking. I flew my 1964 Cessna 205 and three of us to Larry Mead's remote cabin at Gold King. Hardly a thirty-minute flight south of Fairbanks—it was the only practical way to travel to the hunting lodge since there were no roads, you had to cross lots of tundra, and it was not on a river.

The well-maintained gravel runway was an easy few hundred yards north of the camp in the deep woods. The setting was a rustic log cabin with a sod roof and some hand-hewn outbuildings for tools, snowmachine, and a four-wheeler. Larry, the gracious host, willingly chose the lifestyle and lived there full-time by himself. In subsequent years I would be stranded at Larry's when the runway was covered in Styrofoam snow. Once the aircraft slowed enough, the weight of the plane broke through the surface and acted like flypaper on the tires. I had to use full power to simply taxi to the end of the runway. The next day there were the same impossible conditions. Eventually I acquiesced, grabbed a scoop shovel, and over a ten-hour period, dug out the runway so that I could take off. It was backbreaking work, but I was happy the aircraft was still intact.

My first moose hunt in Alaska, a spine shot with my .357 pistol
(not shown) at one hundred meters. It's a long story why the rifle
was not at all effective! Photo by John Pierce.

Col Carson was my partner in the airplane, Paul Fernholtz was a
pharmacist from the clinic where I worked, and his friend that I will
call Russell—I had never met Russell before, but he fancied himself
as a bow hunter, and that's what he was going to carry during rifle
moose-hunting season. Did I mention that I didn't know him from
Adam?

After a big breakfast the next morning, I set out to the southwest
and hunted through the tundra and forest for the lion's share of the
day. I only wore my army field jacket and carried some power bars
and a pint of water along with my Weatherby 30.06. Late that
afternoon I ran into Russell, and we decided to hunt together. We
headed off in an easterly direction, and just prior to dusk, I found my
target and made a single shot-kill from 75 yards. The big bull moose
did not even take one step; the shot was to the heart. Yes, this is how
an Alaskan hunt was supposed to go down. I was confident that my
nearby hunting partner heard the shot and would show up to help
me field dress the mammoth animal. I reloaded my rifle and kept it

within reach while I started the task of both gutting and skinning the large beast. After dark was when I had to be extremely vigilant for the threat of grizzly bears. Any bear within miles would be attracted to the very large and steamy gut pile!

As I worked into the darkness, no one came, but my night vision was more than adequate for the job, and I was happy to be working alone. The gut pile was huge, somewhat difficult to slog around, and a big olfactory welcome mat for any carnivorous predators downwind. I would work on one limb at a time and then one whole side of the animal; I stopped frequently to listen for intruders and sharpen my trusty Buck skinning knife. I made steady progress in the remote Alaskan forest. By 9:00 p.m., my work was finished, and I had started a signal fire. As darkness fell on my kill, so did wet snow.

I paced myself, but it was a bit trickier to start a fire in wet snowy conditions. First I cleared an area to build the fire on the snow. Next I gathered branches on which to build the fire. Now in a timely fashion I had to gather dry kindling from deep inside the evergreens. Protected by branches, desiccated dry moss around the tree trunk would be enough to ignite small green branches, and then the flammable pitch would light larger branches for a nice fire. The real work was in feeding the flames; it was a continuous effort, but did help pass the time. I had no ax, so I was only able to procure small branches and sticks that were quickly consumed in the flames.

Around 10:00 p.m., suddenly lights appeared two hundred yards away. Bouncing through the tundra, it was a four-wheeler headed directly at me. At last I thought the signal fire had paid dividends. I directed my attention to the blaze and prepared to welcome my liberator. In minutes I expected to be speaking with my ride, but as I looked back to where the lights had been—nothing. It was as if I had imagined it. How could I have let my guard down? I could have easily fired a signal shot or, in retrospect, shot the driver. Did he see my fire and was going back for additional help? That didn't make sense. It took the rest of the night for me to answer that question.

About five in the morning, I gave up the vigil and headed back to the cabin. I was more than a little miffed at the night's events; I arrived at 7:00 a.m., just as everyone was finishing a hearty breakfast in the dry, warm cabin. I didn't know why, but I was not really that hungry. I had some coffee, explained the night's events, and told the group where the meat was waiting for them to be picked up. I was not fit to return to the kill site and lay down. "I do not feel well." Russell did not have a reasonable explanation of why he failed to continue the search; secretly I wanted to strangle him. It was unbelievable that he denied seeing my signal fire in the darkness. Why would you want to piss off anyone carrying a 30.06? Was he blind and stupid? I was livid. If I only had the energy, I wanted to kick his ass. It had been twenty-four hours of strenuous work trudging through the tundra and snow with no water then singlehandedly cleaning and skinning a 1,200-pound moose. Unwittingly I had pushed the envelope and was feeling the worse for wear.

The day dawned clear, and many hands made quartering and preparing the moose for transport back into town quick work. I was able to make multiple flights back to Fairbanks with meat and passengers. I remember putting the airplane in the hangar and telling my wife, Cathy, that I did not feel well. I was in no condition to attend the butcher shop with my teammates. I had a bowl of chicken noodle soup and tried to go to bed. Later that evening, my temperature was 105° in my withered condition. Ruth Carson and Cathy returned from packaging the moose and prepared my ice bath—yes, it is what I needed. I was miserable. They both sat in the bathroom while I was in the tub as if joking with me in the field of icebergs was the recommended treatment. My humor just wasn't up to their expectations. I was just plain irritable; you would have been too!

After three liters of fluid and a CT scan the next day, I was hospitalized for a pelvic phlegmon (a purulent inflammation and infiltration of local connective tissue). It was secondary to the severe lack of fluid that my prostate became infected, which spread locally into my pelvis. I was, in fact, septic and would have died if I had not been treated with appropriate IV antibiotics. I continued the IV treatment at home for a total of ten days for a full recovery. For years I carried Septra DS anytime I traveled anywhere. I have had two recurrences of acute bacterial prostatitis since then. However because of my high index of suspicion, I have been able to be treated early with minimal sequelae. Thankfully these episodes were unrelated to climbing.

Now I live in a desert where everyone is prone to dehydration. I moved from Salt Lake City where the average rainfall was twelve inches to Fairbanks, where the annual total precipitation was eleven inches in 1983. Today the Phoenix average rainfall is nine inches. No wonder I love to summer in Coronado, California, so much; I know my skin does.

This is the age of the Camelback, and proper hydration is in the forefront. Just go to REI or Sports Authority to check out the array of power-drink mixes and electrolyte replacements. The military has also addressed this issue in the Middle East with similar hydration systems. For technical climbing, they have built a hydration bladder into a rack (a shoulder sling that climbing gear is clipped onto) for hydration while climbing. Now with a little planning, there is no excuse to deny yourself adequate fluids. The body is up to 75 percent water for a reason. It takes fluid for even the most basic body functions right down to the cellular level. So the next time you want to kill your climbing or hunting partner, he's not going to fall for your ploy so easily.

The Last Word

Over time, readers have remarked to me that I must have my own archangel or nine lives. Indeed I have been most fortunate to have survived so many remarkable experiences. How lucky can one person be? In response, my philosophy has been a conscious desire to live extremes. Not necessarily taking risks, but if the journey passes close to the razor's edge, then so be it. The more varied participation in events or activities, the fuller my life. Influences reflected in these stories include interest in skydiving, ice climbing, flying in the Arctic, training as an Army Special Forces medic, an iron worker on a 550-foot chimney, and mountaineering above 20,000 feet. My residences have spanned from the Nebraska farm to Fort Apache, the Bronx, from the Alaskan "bush" to Europe and Arizona. Each experience, when finally distilled, has shaped me into my collective thought process. We are, in fact, a summation of our accumulative decisions.

Now because you're reading this, you also must be lucky. You too have been graced by democratic freedom and the gift of literacy. Whether this luck is divine or constitutional, we owe it to the soldiers and saints who came before us. Together, we must actively maintain these hard-earned freedoms for the next generation. It was Benjamin Franklin that explained the type of government that was formed following the signing of the Constitution, "A republic, if you can keep it."

Democracies self-destruct when the nonproductive majority realizes that it can vote itself handouts from the productive minority by electing the candidate promising the most benefits from the public treasury. To maintain their power, these candidates must adopt an ever-increasing tax and spend policy to satisfy the increasing desires of the majority. As taxes increase, the incentive to produce decreases, causing many of the once-productive to drop out and join the nonproductive. When there are no longer enough producers to fund the legitimate functions of government and the socialist programs, the democracy will collapse. A dictatorship follows.

All the adult males where I grew up served in the armed forces during WWII. I knew neighbors who were fighter pilots, B-17 tail gunners, and Pearl Harbor survivors, but like my father most were infantry. We should all focus on the difference between a republic and a democracy and how it was paid for with the lives of fellow countrymen that made this an *exceptional country.* Now that the polarizing force of the Cold War is well over, we are engaged in fighting terrorism. Not that we should be hawkish, but rather, those who forget the past are doomed to repeat it. In closing, please reflect on the immortal words of President Abraham Lincoln, "This nation under God is *of* the people, *by* the people, and *for* the people." Each and every American has a duty to preserve what was given to us by our fathers to hand down intact to the next generation. This is the sesquicentennial of the Gettysburg Address written in blood; it is an integral part of the heritage of each American citizen. We must reread these sacred words frequently as a reminder:

> Fourscore and seven years ago our fathers brought forth on this continent a new nation, conceived in liberty and dedicated to the proposition that all men are created equal. Now we are engaged in a great civil war, testing whether that nation or any nation so conceived and so dedicated can long endure. We are met on a great battlefield of that war. We have come to dedicate a portion of that field as a final resting-place for those who here gave their lives that that nation might live. It is altogether fitting and proper that we should do this. But in a larger sense, we cannot dedicate, we cannot consecrate, we cannot hallow this ground. The brave men, living and dead who struggled here have consecrated it far above our poor power to add or detract. The world will little note nor long remember what we say here, but it can never forget what they did here. It is for us the living rather to be dedicated here to the unfinished work which they who fought here have thus far so nobly advanced. It is rather for us to be here dedicated to the great task remaining before us—that

from these honored dead we take increased devotion to that cause for which they gave the last full measure of devotion—that we here highly resolve that these dead shall not have died in vain, that this nation under God shall have a new birth of freedom, and that government of the people, by the people, for the people shall not perish from the earth. (Abraham Lincoln, Nov. 19, 1863)

About the Author

Randy Lippincott was born and raised on a farm in Nebraska. He attended a one-room country schoolhouse until the ninth grade. Lippincott was trained as a Special Forces medic in the army during the Vietnam era. He started skydiving in 1969 and made one thousand free falls (both demonstration and competition) in Europe while serving with the Seventh Army Parachute Team 1971-72. Randy began flying airplanes when he was sixteen years old and has been at it for forty-seven years. He took a four-year hiatus from orthopedic surgery in Alaska and flew five thousand hours as a bush pilot. His initial operating experience was flying with Ryan Air out of Kotzebue, Alaska, on the Bering Sea the winter of 1989. Ultimately he earned his multiengine Airline Transport Pilot certificate and flew the Piper Navajo Chieftain.

After moving to Salt Lake City, Utah, Randy started downhill skiing in 1974. His first NASTAR medal was bronze that same year. He earned a silver medal in 1999 and gold in 2007. His fastest recorded downhill speed was 66.3 mph; his greatest cumulative total for one day documented on his Epic Pass was 61,668 cumulative vertical feet in 2013.

Randy started rock climbing in the Wasatch during 1975 with Terry Loboschefsky and ice climbing in 1976. He graduated from the University of Utah, Physician Assistant program in 1976 when it was a pilot program. Randy graduated from the postgraduate surgical residency program at Montefiore in the Bronx in 1980. Following that, he went back and earned his BS in health science from the University of Utah in 1983 and a master's degree in 1999 from the University of Nebraska while working at Mayo Clinic, Scottsdale, Arizona.

His other interests are sailing, kayaking, fly-fishing, hunting, shooting and reloading, mountain biking, rollerblading, cross-country skiing, downhill skiing, water skiing, photography, woodworking, and flying his own airplane throughout Alaska and the intermountain west.

Twenty-Five Things You Didn't Know About Me

1. The first character I played was Pappy Yokum in my high school play, *Li'l Abner*.
2. My first gun was given to me at age ten. I learned the rules of handling a firearm early and only had to ask permission prior to taking the gun hunting or shooting anytime I wanted. I was told, "Just remember what's behind your target, we don't want you to shoot a neighbor or your brother."
3. I purchased my first muscle car when I was in the eighth grade. My older brother was my partner in the car (because he had a driver's license)—a 1960 red Ford Starliner, 3-speed Hurst on the floor, 352-cubic-inch 4-barrel Holly carburetor, and Astro Mag wheels.
4. I have reloaded my own ammunition since 1976.
5. Sailing is a passion of mine. One day I hope to earn a captain's license.
6. My uncle was killed as a sophomore in high school playing football; however, I played all four years in high school and two weeks in college.
7. I wrestled my senior year. I held the fastest pin in modern school history for many years and earned the very first medal at our first invitational meet at the 133-pound weight class in 1967.
8. I attended a one-room country schoolhouse (built in the 1870s) until my freshman year in high school. The greatest number of pupils for those nine years was twenty-three, and the least was thirteen. I only had one other classmate for most of the time but graduated with Dwayne Randall and Shirley Heule. We hand pumped our water out of the ground outdoors, and there were two outhouses—one for boys and one for girls.
9. Started flying when I was sixteen years old and hope to apply for the Wright Brothers Master Pilot Award on my fiftieth flying anniversary in 2016.

10. I learned to skydive on the same airfield that Charles Lindbergh made his first three jumps. It was Arrow Field on North 48th Street in Lincoln, Nebraska.

11. I built a tabletop loom at age ten and wove many yards of fabric with it.

12. I worked as an operating-room technician at St. Mark's Hospital prior to attending Physician Assistant school at the University of Utah in Salt Lake City in 1974.

13. I downed my first moose with a single shot from my Colt .357 magnum pistol at one hundred yards and climbed Mount McKinley the first year I lived in Alaska.

14. I made one thousand free falls with the 7th Army Parachute Team in Europe. My highest jump was from 19,400 feet out of a UH-1H Huey helicopter. During the 1972 season, I competed on the international circuit. I participated in Tahlequah, Oklahoma, at the 1973 US National Parachuting Championships.

15. I have been employed as a farmer, a painter, a carpenter, a laborer, an iron worker (red iron and rebar), an operating room technician, a Physician Assistant, a soldier, and an airline pilot, worked in a body shop, was a professional free fall exhibitionist, instructed skydiving, and sold real estate.

16. A redhead (Gail) gave me my first broken bone in grammar school.

17. I flew five thousand hours in four years in Alaska as an air taxi (bush) pilot 1989-93.

18. My father set me out starting at age ten to plow fields with a D-4 Caterpillar.

19. I was the first boy in my high school to take home economics as a senior in high school.

20. I started independent horseback riding prior to age five. The horse would fully cooperate; Silver would lower his head so that I could place a bridle on him and throw one rein at a time over his mane. I would lead him over to the corral fence, climb the fence, and leap over onto his bare back. Then I would grab a nap of mane with my left hand and the reins in my right. Silver knew what to do.

21. My second broken bone was a distal ulna and radius fracture when I wrecked my bike trying to jump a twenty-four-inch log at top speed in our gravel driveway.
22. I worked construction on a composite crew building a 550-foot power plant chimney with my brother Jerry.
23. While living in Alaska, it was tradition to fly my airplane around Mount McKinley on New Year's Day—usually at the 14,000-foot level.
24. I wintered in Aviano Italy (1971-72) to facilitate year-round skydiving with the 7th Army Parachute Team, but refused to snow ski with the other guys because I could not risk breaking a leg.
25. I wouldn't trade having grown up on the farm for anything in the world.

The Players in Alphabetical Order

Sam Anderson—My twenty-three-year-old nephew from Cedar Rapids, Iowa. Recent graduate from college in 2010 and was working as night manager for a local Target store. Sam is athletic and an all-around adventure junkie.

Dave Bjorkman—Ice-climbing partner from Salt Lake City and self-described vagabond. Currently he lives in Homer, Alaska.

Cole Carson—My partner in the Cessna 205 and a physical therapist from Fairbanks, Alaska.

Yvon Chouinard—Chouinard was one of the leading climbers of the Golden Age of Yosemite Climbing. He was the founder of Pacific Iron Works and Patagonia clothing.

Mike Covington—Owner of Fantasy Ridge mountain-climbing guide service. He was once a singer and songwriter. Joni Mitchell wrote "Michael from Mountains" in 1967 for him.

Glenn Elison—Outdoorsman and manager of the Arctic National Wildlife Refuge from Fairbanks, Alaska.

Andy Embic, MD—A world-class climber and kayaker. He was a family practice doctor from Valdez, Alaska, and host to the annual Valdez Ice Climbing Festival. The late Andy Embic's home was always open to climbers.

John Gill—Master of Rock, he is the father of modern-day bouldering, an athletic gymnast that fine-tuned the art of powerful difficult moves.

Peter Hackett, MD—Mountaineer and executive director of the Institute for Altitude Medicine. Dr. Hackett has published over one hundred papers related to altitude medicine and has edited eight books.

Martin Leonard III—Bodybuilder, climber, and schoolteacher. Currently he works as Manager at the Kuskokwim River Watershed Council and lives in Bethel, Alaska.

Terry "Lobo" Loboschefsky—My first climbing partner. We left skydiving together in 1975 to teach each other how to rock climb. I owe my start in climbing and love of the technical rock-climbing sport to Lobo. I quite possibly owe my life to his good judgment and practicing the basics of the sport early on. One of the first mantras he taught me was "There are old climbers and there are bold climbers, but there are no old bold climbers!" On Friday night, Lobo called me in Spanish Fork and told me that he had signed us up for an ice-climbing class. I thought he had lost his mind. What was he thinking? On the drive into Salt Lake the next morning, I had to stop for gas. Admittedly I was anxious and thinking about the upcoming class when I drove off with the gas hose still in my tank. Oops, oh well. I returned it to the young man at the Circle K. He just stood there with his mouth hanging open as I departed. It turned out Dean Hannibal at Timberline Sports on Foothill Drive was a good instructor. Saturday we were fitted with gear and learned the French technique on the Great White Icicle in Big Cottonwood Canyon. On Sunday, we practiced on the vertical ice of the apron on Stairway to Heaven in Provo Canyon. It was the beginning of a love affair.

Jeff Lowe—Credited for bringing ice climbing from Europe to America, he has had over one thousand first ascents and is a well-known American alpinist from Ogden, Utah. He introduced ice climbing to the Winter X Games and started the Ouray Ice Festival.

Randy McGregor, MD—A Mayo Clinic-trained anesthesiologist retired from Fairbanks Memorial Hospital. My climbing and hunting partner during the eleven years I lived in Fairbanks, Alaska.

Larry Mead—Owner of the remote log cabin at Gold King, Alaska. Larry lived a true subsistence lifestyle in the wilds of the unspoiled Alaskan wilderness.

Matt Peres—Worked in sales for Cloud Computing and is an accomplished all-around rock and ice climber from Colorado.

Royal Robbins—Famous American mountaineer and rock climber with many first ascents to his credit. Born in California, Robbins is an author, pioneer rock climber, and kayaker.

Jim Sowden—Worked in construction management at Pulte Homes in Phoenix, Arizona, and is an active skydiver and pilot. I introduced him into bouldering, trad climbing, and aviation.

Steve Steckmyer—Had done most of his climbing in the Northwest, Nepal, and Alaska. He was retired as a design engineer for Boeing in Seattle. We attended Central City High School together and entered the army in 1969 under the buddy system. We separated after three months when he fractured his femur during a night jump on the 24th of December 1969. Steve was a man of many talents: motocross, sailing, parasailing, skiing, mountaineering, and he was a fixed-wing pilot. He flew his own home-built aircraft. He suffered a fatal heart attack in 2010 after he had hiked his favorite hill to go parasailing with his good friend Ray Kehl.

Mugs Stump—Famous American mountaineer, perished in a crevasse fall in Alaska in 1992. "Mugs was the complete climber, adept at all forms of the game. Both a dedicated athlete and a seeker after a higher truth beyond the physical manifestations of his sport, he saw climbing as a celebration of boldness, purity, and simplicity."[7]

Kalvan Swanky—Works out in the gym to condition for trad climbing. He loves the challenge of the out-of-doors and had a long tick list of favorite epic climbs and venues. He enjoys mountain biking, skiing, and ice climbing. Always ready for a good time, he is master of the cool.

Carl Tobin—An associate professor of environmental science and outdoor studies at Alaska Pacific University, Anchorage. Carl loves Alaska and enjoys exploring the state through serious alpine-style climbing, extended wilderness bike rides, and mountain biking. In 1996, he was part of a group that made the first full-length traverse (775 miles) of the Alaska Range from Canada to Lake Clark by mountain bike and packraft in forty-two days.

Bradford Washburn—An early mountaineer, world-famous photographer, and cartographer. He made first ascents on the north ridge of Mount Hayes in 1941 and the West Buttress of Mount McKinley in 1951. The late Washburn established the

Boston Museum of Science. He is also honored by the American Mountaineering Museum in Golden, Colorado.

John Waterman—A legend in Alaskan solo climbing, he died in an apparent unwitnessed crevasse fall.

Mark Wumkes—A sailor, climber, and tradesman from Fairbanks, Alaska. He contracted for PICO (polar ice core project) helping design and built the drilling apparatus. Mark was a member of the Alaskan Alpine Club. He had climbed in Alaska for ten years and had made sixteen successful trips to the Alaska Range for a total of 360 days prior to 1987. Mark climbed Denali solo in 1983 and made a four-thousand-mile canoe trip to Alaska in 1978.

Ray Yip—A pediatric hematologist at the Center for Disease Control and my tent mate for seventeen days while on Mount McKinley.

Glossary

4H—Stands for head, heart, hands, and health. It is a structured learning program for youth groups. Used to expose boys and girls to all types of responsible activities: cooking, science, and raising livestock are some examples done with adult mentoring.

Abseil—To use the body or a mechanical device for a brake to slide down a rope in a controlled fashion. Often the most dangerous exercise for a climber as the last one to abseil is without the possibility of a belay. See also *rappel*.

Acclimatization—The gradual adaptation of the human body to the thin air at altitude.

Adze—The hatchet-like blade (turned 90 degrees to the handle) on an ice axe used for cutting steps.

Aid climb—Using artificial anchors or bolts with attached slings or ladders to ascend a featureless rock face.

Alpenglow—Refers to the salmon color cast on the mountains, an optical phenomenon generated following sunset or just prior to sunrise.

Alpine ice—Ice formed in a gully by compacted snow over time; by contrast, hard water ice is a frozen waterfall.

Alpine start—An early-morning (2:00 or 3:00 a.m.) approach to avoid soft snow and avalanche or so that the climber may gain the summit and will be well on his way down to minimize his exposure to afternoon storms and lightning.

Alpine style—Lightweight fast climbing in high mountains, often on ice or snow, to take advantage of good weather conditions and stability of terrain.

Altimeter—A barometric device used to read height and predict weather.

Altitude sickness—A pathological effect of high elevation on humans caused by acute exposure to low partial pressure of oxygen at high altitude. It commonly occurs above eight thousand feet. Acute mountain sickness can progress to high-altitude pulmonary edema (HAPE) or high-altitude cerebral edema (HACE), which are both potentially fatal.

Anchor—Artificial or natural point of attachment for ropes or slings.

Angle of repose—The theoretical angle where the forces that promote stability in the mass of loose rocks (scree) are in balance with the force of gravity weighting the mass downward. The climber's weight may add enough instability to trigger a rockslide.

Apogee—The absolute highest point in the arc of a missile, thrown rock, or body.

Approach—The portion of a climb (usually a trail) leading up to the technical section.

Arête—A fin or narrow vertical ridge on a rock face or prominence.

Ascender—See *Jumar* or *prusik knot.*

Ataxia—An unsteady balance.

Avalanche—The precipitous movement down the slope of a previously stationary mass of snow, rock, mud, or some combination. It may be spontaneous or triggered by the weight of a person.

Avalanche beacon—A radio transceiver used to locate avalanche victims (carrying another beacon switched to transmit) under the snow for rescue or recovery purposes.

Belay—A climber may belay his partner from above or below. The belaying climber feeds the rope through a friction device attached to an anchor or himself to minimize the amount of rope played out in case of a fall by the climber in motion.

Bergschrund—The crevasse that is created where the head of a glacier pulls away from the mountain.

Beta—Information regarding style, sequence, or special secrets to solve a problem.

Big Wall—A tall or long technically demanding route requiring several days to ascend.

Bivouac—Camp out in the open overnight; often it is not planned.

Bivy bag—A lightweight waterproof sack to protect your sleeping bag from moisture and cold, used in place of a tent.

Blitzkrieg—Lightning-like, rapid, or speedy in nature.

Bollard—A snow or ice mushroom fashioned by the climber and normally used as a rappel anchor. At the end of a double-rope rappel, the climber pulls on one end of the cord to recover it for repeated use.

Bolt—A substantial threaded metal pin drilled into the rock to provide a permanent anchor. A hanger is secured to the threaded bolt by a nut to accept a carabiner.

Bolt ladder—A series of fixed hangers (bolts) within reach of each other that can be used to scale a smooth vertical or overhanging face by progressively clipping into a higher bolt to support climbing.

Bomber placement—Extremely secure protection.

Bouldering—To climb a short but difficult rock, wall, or building unprotected by rope or harness. A fall typically is of little consequence.

Cairn—A stack of native rock or wood to mark a trail. Cairns are usually placed at an interval so they are within sight of each other or marking an obvious trail.

Chalk bag—Climbers may use gymnastic chalk (magnesium carbonate) to dry their hands for better friction or grip on the rock carried in a small reusable sack at the waist.

Chickenhead—A protruding clump of contrasting rock or stony boss (usually granite) used as a hand or foothold.

Chimneying—Climbing a large crack or fissure using an opposing foot-and-back technique on opposite walls. Often can be very strenuous, especially with a pack.

Carabiner—An oval or D-shaped metal ring with a swinging or locking gate used to quickly connect rope or webbing to a bolt (with a hanger) or any other miscellaneous device.

Chock—A metal nut on a rope or wire used for protection when placed in a crack.

Chockstone—A boulder or rock naturally wedged in a chimney or crack.

Classic route—An aesthetic climb or route of any grade that has gained popularity due to its history, location, or outstanding quality.

Clean the pitch—When the lead climber has reached the end of the rope or stopped at a strategic place on the climb and has placed anchors, he belays the second climber up to his position. As the second climbs, he stops at each placement of protection and removes it to be reused, thereby "cleaning" the pitch. He leaves the rock face unchanged by his passage.

Clipping in—To use a carabiner to connect the rope to "pro" or attach a climber to an anchor.

Col—A ridge (smaller than a saddle) between two peaks.

Committing—A climb or move that is very difficult or impossible to retreat from.

Cornice—A well-formed wind-sculpted lip or drift of snow flowing from a ridge or surface that may vary in size. It appears to be a cresting wave that has been frozen in time. Walking on top of one can be extremely dangerous. The climber may plunge through it into space or the entire mass of snow may break off due to the climber's weight.

Couloir—A steep mountainside gully or chute filled with snow and or ice.

Crags—Typically a British term referring to a steep rocky area used for climbing.

Crampons—Metal cages with down—and front-pointing spikes that strap onto the stiff climbing boot to ascend steep snow and vertical ice.

Crash pad—A bouldering mat placed on the ground to break the climber's fall. It may be used in conjunction with a spotter, a person on the ground that may direct the climber's body toward the pad.

Crevasse—A crack or fissure in a glacier potentially covered by snow and is a serious fall hazard for climbers traveling on glaciers.

Crown wall—The well-defined vertical face (from inches to many feet) at which point a slab avalanche breaks free from a slope. The taller the crown wall, the greater the volume and destructive forces of the avalanche.

Crux—The point that a climb reaches its maximal difficulty.

Cyclorama—A large composite picture placed on the inside walls of a round room so as to appear in 360 degrees. It usually tells a story and is seen as from a natural perspective to a spectator in the center of the room.

Deadman—An anchor buried in the snow, usually a picket or shovel like device.

Descender—Used as a friction device to safely slide or rappel down a rope.

DEW line—A perimeter of interlocking over the horizon radars to detect an aerial attack during the cold war, **D**istant **E**arly **W**arning system.

Dinner plate—When extremely cold hard ice is struck with an ice axe, a concave area about the size of a dinner plate (twelve to fourteen inches across) may typically explode outward and away from the point of impact, rendering the effort useless. A second blow in the same spot usually provides a secure purchase with the axe.

Donner party—A wagon train of eighty-seven pioneers who were caught in a mountainous blizzard in northern Nevada during 1846. The surviving members resorted to well documented cannibalism.

Down climb—A good practice exercise for climbers; however, it is more difficult to down climb a route, but it is safer than rappelling when time permits.

Dry-tool—To climb a section of rock using an ice axe and crampons.

Edging—A rock-climbing technique using the stiff edges of climbing shoes to gain a purchase on small footholds. See also *smearing*.

Entropy—The physical nature dictating that mater is constantly in a state of decay.

Epistaxis—A nosebleed.

Exposure—The greatest distance the climber would travel if his fall was unchecked.

Fall—To involuntarily slip off or pop loose from the rock or ice. A whipper or a screamer is long enough to provoke a guttural response from the falling victim.

Fall line—The path a snowball would take if let go down a slope. The direction a fall would travel on a vertical face.

FBO—Fixed base operator. It's like a service station for airplanes.

Finger locks—A means of placing or stacking two or more fingers in a crack, torquing in a cam-like motion to gain traction to pull one's self up or into the rock while climbing.

Fist jam—To place your flat hand in a crack and make a fist to generate enough pressure on the rock to hang your body weight on your arm. A technique used to scale rock faces.

Fixed rope—A static or dynamic climbing rope anchored into the rock, snow, or ice to be used by multiple people over a period of time. It may be left in place for the season or the duration of a certain climb.

Flagging—A technique where the leg is held in a position to maintain balance rather than to support weight.

Fluke—A snow anchor or shovel like device that is driven deeper into the snow when force is applied to it in a dynamic fashion.

Formication—Irritable, twitchy, prickly sensation, a feeling of small insects crawling under the skin.

Fourteener—A 14,000-foot or taller mountain peak.

Free climb—Using only hands and feet for an ascent. A rope is typically employed for safety. See also *aid climbing*.

Free solo—Climbing rock without any means of protection or security; if the climber were to fall it would be certain death.

French Technique—Walking flat-footed with crampons on ice or snow, usually sideways with the toes pointing downslope and using an ice axe for balance. See also *pied à plat*.

Front pointing—ice climbing vertical or overhanging ice with 12-point crampons—the forward points of the crampon provide a purchase on the vertical ice for the feet.

Gaston—A climbing grip using one hand with the thumb down and elbow out. The grip maintains friction against a hold by pressing outward toward the elbow.

Gendarme—French for *police*; in climbing it is a pinnacle of rock protruding up from a ridge (guarding against further progress) that may cause the climber to circumvent it rather than climb over it.

Glissade—French, to ski down a slope standing up on your feet with no special equipment; in other words, no skis are used.

Grade—The difficulty assigned to a particular climb. See Yosemite Decimal System explained.

Haboob—Monstrous dust storm that approaches with an imposing wall of dirt.

Hand jam—Stacking one hand on the other to gain traction in a crack to facilitate climbing. See also *fist jam*.

Hanger—A stout metal plate bent 90 degrees with holes in both ends. One hole is round and accepts a bolt to fasten it to the rock with a nut, and the other hole is oval to accept a carabiner. See also *bolt*.

Hard water ice—Vertical ice formed by a frozen waterfall; by contrast, alpine ice is formed over time in a gully by compacted snow or by a thaw/freeze cycle.

Headwall—The steep upper section of the mountain that is set off from the lower, less severe portion.

High-ball bouldering—A tall risky boulder problem, usually anything over 7 meters or 23 feet in height. Falling becomes more dangerous due to the increase in height.

Hypoxia—Suboptimal level of oxygen in the blood associated with high altitude, often associated with poor judgment.

Hypothermia—Low body core temperature, starting at 95° F. The major cause of death in the wilderness.

Ice ax—A mountaineering tool, a pick and adze on one end and pointed on the other end of the shaft. Used for ice climbing and mountaineering.

Ice hammer—A similar tool as the ice ax; however, the adze is replaced by a hammerhead for pounding in pitons and other protection.

Ice screw—A threaded (on the outside) hollow tube (smooth on the inside) for boring into ice and is used as an anchor while ice climbing.

IFR—Instrument Flight Rules. These are well-established procedures for flying in the clouds or without reference to the ground.

Igneous—One of the three main rock types—the others are sedimentary and metamorphic. Igneous rock is formed through the cooling and solidification of magma or lava from the earth's core.

Jumar or clog—A mechanical device or pair of devices used to ascend a rope.

Kernmantle rope—The inner core or kern provides the tensile strength; the outer core or mantle is a woven sheath that provides strength, durability, and flexibility along with abrasion resistance.

Klepper—A collapsible seagoing kayak that can be broken down and placed in two duffel bags for transportation; they come in one— and two-man versions.

Lead—To climb with the rope trailing behind you. If the leader should fall, the radius of his fall is the distance back to his last piece of protection that the rope is running through.

Lieback—A technique used along a crack or sharp edge of rock where the climber's hands both pull one direction and his feet push the opposite for traction to ascend the route.

Malebolge—The eighth circle of hell in Dante's *Inferno*, pronounced "malbowges." Translated from Italian, Malebolge means "evil ditches." Malebolge is a large, funnel-shaped cavern divided into ten concentric circular trenches or ditches. Each trench is called a *bolgia* (Italian for "pouch" or "ditch"). The eighth is one of the worst to occupy.

Mantel—A move used to surmount a ledge or feature in the rock in the absence of any useful holds directly above. It involves pushing down on a ledge or feature instead of pulling down. In ice climbing, a mantel is done by moving the hands from the shaft to the top of the ice tool and pushing down on the head of the tool.

Micturate—The act of urination.

Mixed climbing—A route that ascends any combination of rock, ice, or snow.

Moraine—The debris consisting of all sizes of rocks and boulders deposited at the tongue of a glacier (the terminal moraine). When rocks are deposited on the side, it is a lateral moraine.

MSR fuel bottle—A company, Mountain Safety Research, that manufactures camping and outdoor equipment.

Multipitch climb—A technical climb consisting of more than a single pitch or rope length—about 150 feet.

Natural doping—Because of the decreased amount of oxygen in the air at high altitudes, red blood cell production is physiologically stimulated so as to be able to carry more available oxygen to the brain and muscles. It takes about 2 days for the body to start to stimulate the production of RBCs. The lifespan of a RBC is normally 120 days.

Nunatak—A mountain or solitary rock that protrudes through an ice field.

Nut—A metallic stopper or metal wedge with a loop of cable or rope threaded through it to be lodged into a crack as a piece of protection. It is removed by the last climber on the pitch.

Off-width—A crack that is larger than the hand or foot to jam into but too small for the body to fit into. Typically awkward and difficult to climb.

On sight—To smoothly complete a climb with no prior knowledge of the moves or difficulty.

Phlegmon—An infection of local connective tissue that is about to be transformed into a pus-filled abscess.

Pied à main—A movement where the foot is placed on the same hold as the hand.

Pied à plat—A crampon technique in the French style: to climb on high-angle ice with feet flat on the ice (as opposed to front-pointing). See also *French Technique.*

Pitch—A rope length or section of climb to be done in one continuous lead, typically about 100-150 feet between belay points.

Piton—An iron or steel peg or spike to be driven into a crack to act as an anchor to aid in climbing or to provide security. It may or may not be removed, but it does deface the rock over time.

Postprandial somnolence—Blood is involuntarily shunted to the gut following a meal; this deprives oxygen to the brain and makes one sleepy after eating.

Pro placement—Using various mechanical devices like cams, but including pitons, to be wedged into cracks or slings placed around stony bosses (chickenheads) to act as an anchor to catch the leader's fall. The distance the leading climber is above the last placement of "pro" would be the radius of his fall.

Protection—See *pro placement.*

Prusik—Several loops of a small diameter rope around a larger-diameter rope used as a sliding friction knot used to ascend an anchored rope. See *jumar* or *clog.*

Purulent—Refers to an infection, pus, or exudate, typically white to yellow. Signifies that a bacteria is present.

Quickdraw—Two carabiners linked together with a short but strong strap, used to clip a climbing rope to a hanger or "pro" in sport climbing.

Rack—A sling over a climber's shoulder or harness loops on which various pieces of protection for a given climb are organized.

Rampart—An earthen or stone embankment or cliff. French for "fortification."

Rappel—To use the body or a mechanical device for a brake or friction device to slide down a rope in a controlled fashion. Often the most dangerous exercise for a climber as the last one to rappel is without the possibility of a belay. See also *abseil.*

Ratings—See explanation of the Yosemite Decimal System.

Redpointing—Completing a climb in good style but only after practice on that climb.

Repose—See *angle of repose.*

Rime ice—A very thin layer of opaque ice formed from supercooled water droplets.

Rubicon—Extremely rugged trail or passage. Once crossed, the traveler is committed irrevocably. Also a river in northern Italy.

Runner—A nylon sling used in combination with "pro" and carabiner used for safety.

Saddle—Or *col,* the lowest point on a ridge between two summits.

Saltation—The skipping motion of a grain of sand caused by wind or water action; on a small scale, it forms riffles and on a large scale, sand dunes.

Scree—Loose small rock or debris on a slope at an angle that is difficult and laborious to ascend.

Second—The number two or lower climber to follow on a pitch that is belayed by the leader from above.

Self-arrest—When an unroped climber falls on a slope usually less than 60 degrees, digs his ice ax into the snow, pivots so that the legs are downhill, draws the ax under the chest area, and slows enough so that he does not flip over when he digs in his toes or crampons to come to a complete stop.

Séracs—Large ice pinnacles formed by glaciers that are in various stages of tumbling down as if on a conveyer belt. This is particularly dangerous for the climber because their collapse is unpredictable.

Sequelae—Unwanted side effects or complications.

Sherpa Tenzing Norgay—One of the most famous mountain climbers in the world. A Nepalese native was the first to reach the summit on Mount Everest along with Sir Edmund Hillary on May 29, 1953.

Sling—Or *nylon runner*. It is a loop of wedding or cord used with carabiners to attach anchors or protection to the climbing rope.

Smearing—To smear while climbing is to apply the greatest area on the sole of the foot to the smooth surface of the rock for the greatest friction.

Snowmachine—The Alaskan term for the snowmobile or iron dog.

Spindrift—Drifting or blowing loose powder snow.

Sport climbing—A climbing route designed to be scaled with minimum gear. Bolts with hangers are permanently placed in the rock at strategic intervals; the leader uses quickdraws to clip the rope to the hangers for safety.

Stem—To bridge the distance between two holds or faces using one's feet in an opposing fashion.

Synergistic—Acting together, the whole is greater than the sum of its parts.

Talus—The product of rockfall over time collecting in a given location, which should be a red flag for the astute climber. You are, in fact, standing in the slide zone. See also *scree*.

Tamponade—The application of pressure on a focal area to stop bleeding.

Technical climbing—Difficult climbing that requires skill and practice to complete. Rope and protection is used for safety.

Tick list—A catalog of desirous climbs that you plan to conquer at some point in the future.

Top-rope—A single-pitch climb in which the belayer and the climber start at the same point. The rope has been preplaced over an anchor (pulley) at the top of the climb, and the belayer remains at the bottom.

Trad climbing—Climbing on a rock face with little or no fixed protection (permanent anchors for belay stations are placed on popular routes) and leaving no signs of your passage, including defacing the rock.

Tremor Land—The movie *Tremors* with Kevin Bacon was shot using this area of boulders near Mount Whitney as background.

Urohydrosis—The act of urinating on oneself for evaporative cooling.

Verglas—A very thin coating or glaze of ice that forms over rocks when rainfall or melting snow freezes. Hard to climb on as crampons have insufficient depth for reliable penetration.

Wag bags—Biodegradable sacks with kitty litter in the bottom to accumulate human waste for disposal at a proper collection point.

Water ice—See *hard water ice*.

Windchill—The difference between the ambient air temperature and effective temperature caused by the result of air moving across exposed skin. The body loses heat through convection, evaporation, conduction, and radiation.

White Spider—The upper snowfield on the North Face of the Eiger in Switzerland. It is fed by multiple runnels of snow that, from a distance, appear to be legs of a spider.

Yosemite Decimal System

The Yosemite Decimal System[8] (YDS) is a three-part system used for rating the difficulty of walks, hikes, and climbs. It is primarily used by mountaineers in the United States and Canada. The Class 5 portion of the Class scale is primarily a rock climbing classification system. Originally the system was a single-part classification system. In recent years, Grade and Protection categories were added to the system. The new categories do not apply to every climb and usage varies widely. While primarily considered a free climbing system, an aid climbing designation is sometimes appended. For example, The North America Wall on El Capitan would be classed "VI, 5.8, A5" using this mixed system.[9]

YDS Class The system was initially developed as the Sierra Club *grading system* in the 1930s to classify hikes and climbs in the Sierra Nevada. Previously, these were described relative to others. For example Z is harder than X but easier than Y. This primitive system was difficult to learn for those who did not yet have experience of X or Y. The club adapted a numerical system of classification that was easy to learn and which seemed practical in its application. Guidebooks often append some number of stars to the YDS rating, to indicate a climb's overall "quality" (how "fun" or "worthwhile" the climb is). This "star ranking" is unrelated to the YDS system, and varies from guidebook to guidebook. The system now divides all hikes and climbs into five classes:[10] The exact definition of the classes is somewhat controversial.[11]

- Class 1: Walking with a low chance of injury.
- Class 2: Simple scrambling, with the possibility of occasional use of the hands. Little potential danger is encountered.
- Class 3: Scrambling with increased exposure. A rope can be carried but is usually not required. Falls are not always fatal.
- Class 4: Simple climbing, with exposure. A rope is often used. Natural protection can be easily found. Falls may well be fatal.
- Class 5: Technical free climbing involving rope, belaying, and other protection hardware for safety. Un-roped falls can result in severe injury or death.

The original intention was that the classes would be subdivided decimally, so that a class 4.5 route would be a climb halfway between 4 and 5. Class 5 was subdivided in the 1950s. Initially it was based on ten climbs of Tahquitz Rock in Idyllwild, California, and ranged from the "Trough" at 5.0, a relatively modest technical climb, to the "Open Book" at 5.9, considered at the time the most difficult unaided climb humanly possible. This system was developed by members of the Rock Climbing Section of the Angeles Chapter of the Sierra Club.[4] Increased standards and improved equipment meant that class 5.9 climbs in the 1960s became only of moderate difficulty for some. Rather than reclassify all climbs each time standards improved, additional classes were added. It soon became apparent that an open-ended system was needed and further classes of 5.11, 5.12, etc. were added. It was later determined that the 5.11 climb was much harder than 5.10, leaving many climbs of varying difficulty bunched up at 5.10. To solve this, the scale has been further subdivided above the 5.9 mark with suffixes from "a" to "d." As of 2005, several climbs are considered to have a difficulty of 5.15a. The original Sierra Club grading system also had a Class 6, for artificial, or aid climbing. This sort of climbing uses ropes and other equipment where progress is made by climbing directly on equipment placed in or on the rock and not the rock itself. Class 6 is no longer widely used. Today aid climbing uses a separate scale from A0 through A5.[12] Classification of climbs between indoor gym, sport and traditional climbing can also vary quite a bit depending on location and history.

The YDS grade system involves an optional Roman numeral grade that indicates the length and seriousness of the route. The grades are:

- Grade I: One to two hours of climbing.
- Grade II: Less than half a day.
- Grade III: Half a day climb.
- Grade IV: Full day climb.
- Grade V: Two day climb.
- Grade VI: Multiday climb.[13]
- Grade VII: A climb lasting a week or longer.

The Grade is more relevant to mountaineering and big wall climbing, and often not stated when talking about short rock climbs.

YDS Protection Rating An optional protection rating indicates the spacing and quality of the protection available for a well-equipped and skilled leader. The letter codes chosen were, at the time, identical to the American system for rating movies:

- G: Good, solid protection.
- PG: Pretty good, few sections of poor or non-existent placements.
- PG13: OK protection, falls may be long but will probably not cause serious injury.
- R: Run out, some protection placements may be very far apart (possibility of broken bones, even when properly protected).
- X: No protection, extremely dangerous (possibility of death even when properly protected).

The G and PG ratings are often left out as they are typical of normal, everyday climbing. R and X climbs are usually noted as a caution to the unwary leader. Application of protection ratings varies widely from area to area and from guidebook to guidebook.

How Much Water Do You Really Need to Drink?[14]

You'd think we were suffering a nationwide drought, the way Americans go around clutching bottles of water these days. Forget American Express cards: The one thing many of us would never dream of leaving home without is our bottled water. By all rights, that should be good news. For years nutritionists have been warning us about the dangers of dehydration. Quaff at least eight 8-ounce glasses of water, the common wisdom goes, or you'll suffer the consequences: flagging energy, dry skin, lowered disease resistance, even constipation. And don't count the coffee, tea, or other caffeinated beverages you drink. Anything with caffeine, we've long been told, actually increases the risk of dehydration because it flushes water out of the system. Nor can you rely on thirst. By the time you're thirsty, you're well on your way to being dehydrated. There's only one problem with all these warnings. Almost none of them hold water. Here's why:

Myth No. 1: We need to drink at least eight 8-ounce glasses of water a day

Researchers aren't sure where this familiar advice came from, but most agree there's very little solid scientific evidence to support it. The average adult loses only about 1 liter of water a day through sweating and other bodily processes—the equivalent of only four 8-ounce glasses. We typically get that much water just in the foods we eat. Drinking an *additional* eight tall glasses of H20 is probably more fluid than most of us need. What about older people? For years, experts have warned that elderly people are especially prone to dehydration because they lose their sense of thirst. But even this may be overstated, according to a report in the July 2000 *Journal of Gerontology*. Robert Lindeman, MD, professor emeritus of medicine at the University of New Mexico, surveyed fluid consumption among 833 elderly volunteers. "People who drank less than four glasses of water a day were no more likely to show signs of dehydration than those who drank six or more," says Lindeman. "We found absolutely no difference between those who drank a little and those who drank a lot when we looked at all the standard markers for dehydration."

Of course, that doesn't mean you *shouldn't* drink plenty of water a day. In fact, there's at least one reason to think it's a very good idea. In a 1999 study published in *The New England Journal of Medicine*, researchers found that the more liquids men consumed, the lower their risk of bladder cancer. Men who drank more than 10 8-ounce servings of fluids had a 49% lower incidence of the disease than those who drank only half that much.

Myth No. 2: Caffeinated beverages make you dehydrated

Not true. "For years, newspaper and magazine articles have repeated the notion that caffeine is dehydrating as if it's absolute fact," says University of Nebraska researcher Ann Grandjean, EdD. But in a study published in the October 2000 *Journal of the American College of Nutrition*, Grandjean and her colleagues at the Center for Human Nutrition showed that it's pure fantasy.

The researchers looked at how different combinations of water, coffee, and caffeinated colas affected hydration levels in a group of 18 men between the ages of 24 and 39. During one phase of the experiment, the only fluid the volunteers consumed was water. During another, 75% of their intake was caffeinated. "Using almost every test ever devised to measure dehydration, we found no difference at all," says Grandjean.

Myth No. 3: By the time you feel thirsty, you're already becoming dehydrated

Maybe if you're an elite athlete running a marathon or a hotshot tennis player sweating in the noonday sun—but not if you're going about your everyday activities.

Thirst is, in fact, a very sensitive mechanism for regulating fluid intake, according to Barbara Rolls, PhD, and a nutrition researcher at Pennsylvania State University. In a 1984 study in *Physiology and Behavior*, she and a group of colleagues at Oxford University followed a group of men as they went through their normal day. Left to their own devices, the volunteers became thirsty and drank long before their hydration levels showed any signs of dipping. Says Rolls, "If people have access to water or other fluid beverages, they seem to do a very good job of maintaining hydration levels."

Myth No. 4: Drinking plenty of water can help you lose weight

This idea makes sense, since water contains no calories. The trouble is, drinking a glass of water doesn't do anything to take the edge off hunger. "Water sneaks right past without triggering satiety signals, the cues that tell your body when you're full," says nutritionist Barbara Rolls, author of *Volumetrics*.

Surprisingly, adding water to the food you eat, on the other hand, does seem to tame hunger. In a study reported in the October 1999 *American Journal of Clinical Nutrition*, Rolls found that women who eat a bowl of chicken soup feel fuller than those who eat chicken casserole served with a glass of water, even though both meals contain exactly the same ingredients. The soup eaters also tended to be less hungry at their next meal—and to consume fewer calories—than those who ate the casserole.

There is one way that drinking water could help you lose weight, however: if you drink it in place of beverages that contain a lot of added sugar. Like water, sugary beverages fail to trigger a sense of fullness, which means you can consume a lot of calories without taking the edge off.

40 Shocking Facts About Water[15]

Water: we once thought it was an endless natural resource. Now we know better.

1. Over 1.5 billion people do not have access to clean, safe water.
2. Almost 4 million people die each year from water related diseases.
3. 43% of these water related deaths are due to diarrhea.
4. 98% of all these water related deaths occur in the developing countries.
5. Unsafe drinking water is responsible for most deaths in children below five; nearly 90% of diarrhea deaths occur in this age group.
6. In the Sub-Saharan region of Africa, women spend at least 16 hours a week collecting drinking water.
7. A typical citizen of the United States uses 500 liters of water on a daily basis.
8. As per the recommended daily water requirement for consumption, cooking, bathing and sanitation is approximately 50 liters for each person every day.
9. More than 1 billion people use less than six liters of water daily.
10. In Gambia, an individual typically uses just 4.5 liters of water each day.
11. Lack of clean water access has claimed more lives through disease than any of the wars fought in the world.
12. The average toilet uses 8 liters of clean water in a single flush.
13. At any one time, more than half the world's poor are ill due to inadequate sanitation, water or hygiene.
14. It takes over 11,000 liters of water to produce a pound of coffee.
15. Half the world's schools do not have access to clean water, nor adequate sanitation.
16. It takes about 300 liters of water to make the paper for just one Sunday newspaper.
17. Agriculture is responsible for about 70% of the world's water usage. Industry uses a further 22%.

18. 443 million school days are lost each year due to water related illness.
19. On average, women in Africa and Asia have to walk 3.7 miles to collect water.
20. The average dishwasher uses over 100 liters per cycle.
21. It takes up to 5,000 liters of water to produce 1 kg of rice.
22. 80% of all illness in the developing world comes from waterborne diseases.
23. Drilling a fresh water well can cost anything from a few hundred dollars to over $40,000.
24. Over 2.6 billion people lack access to adequate sanitation.
25. 90% of wastewater in developing countries is discharged into rivers or streams without any treatment.
26. About 1.8 million child deaths a year are due to diarrhea.
27. An 18 liter can of water weighs 20 kilos.
28. About half the world's hospital beds are occupied by someone with a water related illness.
29. A five minute shower in an American household will use more water than a person living in a developing world slum will use in a whole day.
30. A third of the people without access to clean water live on less than a dollar a day. More than two thirds live on less than two dollars a day.
31. Water consumption in a US household is eight times that of an Indian household.
32. In India alone, waterborne diseases cost the economy 73 million working days per year.
33. In sub-Saharan Africa a child's chance of dying from diarrhea is over 500 times greater than in Europe.
34. Approximately 2.5 billion people lack access to appropriate sanitation facilities.
35. About 1.2 billion people have absolutely no access to a sanitation facility.
36. In a typical year in Africa 510 times the number of people die from diarrhea than from war.

37. Simply washing hands can decrease the chance of diarrhea by around 35%.
38. Global sales of bottled water account for over $60-$80 billion each year.
39. A child dies of waterborne diseases about every 15 seconds (that's about 12 children just since you started reading this article). By this time tomorrow, another 2,500 will be dead.
40. As little as one dollar can provide clean water for a child in the developing world for an entire year.

Endnotes

1   Chris Kyle, *American Sniper* (Deckle Edge 2011).
2   Yvon Chouinard quote, circa 1960s.
3   "Devils Tower National Monument," Native American folklore, *Wikipedia*.
4   Note excerpts by Piero Scaruffi, http://www.scaruffi.com/travel/northfor.html.
5   John Gill, "The Art of Bouldering," *American Alpine Journal* (1969).
6   Los Alamos Mountaineers, "North American Classic Climbs."
7   Michael Kennedy, *Mugs Stump Alpine Climbing Award*, (October 1, 2012). http://mugsstumpaward.com/aboutmugs/
8   "Yosemite Decimal System," *Wikipedia*.
9   Don Reid and Chris Falkenstein, *Rock Climbs of Tuolomne Meadows*, 3rd ed. (Evergreen, Colorado: Chockstone Press, 1992), 129.
10 Steve Roper, *The Climber's Guide to the High Sierra* (Sierra Club Books, 1976), 1921.
11 "The Yosemite Decimal System," Climber.org, retrieved 20090115, http://climber.org/data/decimal.html.
12 *Mountaineering: The Freedom of the Hills*, 6th ed., (Seattle: The Mountaineers.)
13 Eric Bjornstad, *Desert Rock—Rock Climbs in the National Parks* (Evergreen, Colorado: Chockstone Press, 1996), 7.
14 Peter Jaret, *WebMD* feature article (April 16, 2001).
15 Matt Scott, *Matador Network*, (June 30, 2009).

Index